JOYRIDER

JOYRIDER

How Gratitude Can Help You Get
the Life You Really Want

ANGELA SCANLON

Vermilion
LONDON

1

Vermilion, an imprint of Ebury Publishing,
20 Vauxhall Bridge Road,
London SW1V 2SA

Vermilion is part of the Penguin Random House group of companies
whose addresses can be found at global.penguinrandomhouse.com

Angela Scanlon has asserted her right to be identified as the author of this
Work in accordance with the Copyright, Designs and Patents Act 1988

First published in Great Britain by Vermilion in 2022

www.penguin.co.uk

A CIP catalogue record for this book is available from the British Library

ISBN 9781785043895

Printed and bound in Great Britain by Clays Ltd, Elcograf S.p.A.

The authorised representative in the EEA is Penguin Random House Ireland,
Morrison Chambers, 32 Nassau Street, Dublin D02 YH68

MIX
Paper from
responsible sources
FSC
www.fsc.org
FSC® C018179

Penguin Random House is committed to a sustainable
future for our business, our readers and our planet.
This book is made from Forest Stewardship Council®
certified paper.

Contents

To Roy, Ruby and Marnie
My roots and my wings

Well hello, thank you for being here!

There are a million books you could have chosen and here we are. Thank you! I hope you find something here that lovingly kicks you up the arse or gently leads you to unexpected places. Let's go.

Here's my theory ... People are either dogs or cats. Cats are slick and self-assured. They're grounded and confident. They love themselves, which is why many people think they're arrogant. Dogs, on the other hand, will roll over and pant and lick and *need* – they will do anything for you. They will love you forever but often at the expense of themselves.

I am a dog. I wish I was a cat.

Or maybe a Cog – some sort of hybrid animal that was centred enough to love myself but not be a selfish cow. But here's the thing: self-love is not selfish. It's not obnoxious or indulgent; it does not come at the expense of other types of love that are deemed more acceptable. Yes, it's written on t-shirts and mugs and all manner of shite but the act itself is something that can't be bought. Self-love is the start of everything, and without it we are on borrowed time, living a life that's dictated by everyone around us, everyone we are trying to make love us because we can't love ourselves. Loving ourselves comes only when we fully know ourselves, when we're familiar with all the murky, annoying parts too and we accept them, eventually.

I spent 37 years trying to be someone else. Anyone else. Changing by the day, hour, minute. Popping on a new identity, a new opinion, a new approach depending on my company. I was a genius at reading people and stealthily changing tack to be more acceptable, more relaxed, cooler, funnier, more loveable. For a couple of decades now I've been exploring all kinds of self-help stuff, buying anything that promised to fill me up.

There's quite a list ... gong baths, reiki, psych-K, human design, pills, tinctures, homeopathy, traditional therapy, and the rest. Before 'wellness' was a billion-pound business and when Gwyneth was still an actor, I bought all the things, did all of the retreats, and hoped that every potion I ingested, every book I read, would help me feel *fixed*. I'm not sure what I was hoping to 'fix' but I was yearning, often desperately, for a sense of something more, a longing for deeper connection, proper fulfilment, some sort of satisfaction, any satisfaction. I realise I'm talking in the past tense; I still do lots of these things, I am still yearning for deeper connection and my instinct is always for the quick fix. It's ongoing and as soon as I get cocky and complacent, I am walloped around the head with the delightful self-doubt and that gnawing, nagging feeling that has followed me around since I can remember. I am, much to my frustration, not 'fixed'. When I'm under pressure I revert to all my old habits; sometimes it takes me weeks and a flood of tears to remind me I've lost my way again and it feels like I start all over, but each time it's a little easier.

For years I have made lists. Lists of things to do, things I needed to achieve, jobs I needed to get in order to make me feel full. A long-held belief that when I got there, when I did 'that' thing, when I ticked items off the list and arrived at that elusive place in the future (an ever-moving destination), *then* I would be happy. Then I would be whole. But when I did get there – when things I couldn't have imagined got crossed off those dream-lists – I felt hollow and sad, and I was terrified that I was broken; that somewhere along the way I had lost the capacity to have joy in my life. To feel joy on any level. Maybe that circuit in me was faulty; unfortunate and excruciating but something that I might just have to live with. Then I thought, fuck that, this cannot be it. This half-mast existence, the volume turned down, the want always bubbling . . . this cannot be it. Can it? Maybe in a bid at self-preservation or sweet desperation, I started to consider that perhaps it wasn't me that was faulty, but my system. That was the first bit of compassion I had given myself in a while, a glimpse at what 'having my own back' might feel like and the realisation that until this point I had been 'coupled up' with a Mean Girl – myself. Maybe instead of striving to do all the things in the hope that I would somehow satiate the beast for a bit, I would confront her (and give her a hug). I would kill her with kindness or smother her with affection, I would give her love, introduce her to joy and force her to find herself. And so began a slightly different type of search . . .

I do not have the answers. I'm not an expert but I consider myself a human guinea pig, and over the years have built up a toolkit that I return to regularly. The heavier it gets, the lighter I get! I hope that some of the tools inside will work for you too.

Chapter One

In Your Own Company – How Discovering Yourself is the Gateway to Joy

When I became a mother, I finally sat still for the first time in decades and my little world imploded. In a way it was the forced stillness of those early days that got to me. Sitting for hours under a feeding baby, when she finally nodded off, I was afraid to move. For a long time, I was afraid to breathe. I had spent years creating a life that allowed me to run away, to distract myself and fill my ears and mind with noise. Even when I was chilling out, I was overstimulated. Reading a book while on my phone and watching telly at the same time. I was incapable of relaxing or switching off but was completely in denial about that.

I always pitied people who felt uncomfortable having lunch alone; it was one of my favourite things to do except I was never *actually* alone. I was on Instagram and reading a magazine, chatting to a waiter or reading the back of a menu, over and over again. I was technically on my own but not quite. Obsessed with busyness, itchy in silence, proud of my frantic energy and ability to keep going, unaware of its impact on me and everyone around me.

Motherhood might not have been your catalyst; that life change, rock bottom or wake-up call can come in many forms and at different times. There's a chance you may not need one at all and this book is just for fun and you're thinking, 'shit this chick needs to chill out, why can't she just talk about bench seating like usual?' But if you relate to the 'always-on-never-no' vibe, and you're ready for a shift, there is hope!

Wherever I Go, There I Am

I was running away from myself because I was afraid of what I might hear if I slowed down for long enough to listen. Afraid of what would come up when the noise stopped. I didn't want to hear something I knew I couldn't 'unhear'. And that is the frightening thing: the realisation that the voice inside – if you can shut up for a bit – knows you deeply, wants to guide you, wants to support you to become the best version of yourself but that requires knowing all versions of yourself first and embracing yourself, warts and all. It sounds hideous, and at points it is (and so are you; we all are, it's a human thing) but, if you can look at the gremlins within, you'll also see how furry they are, and furry is great in any situation.

When you start to really explore yourself and get to know yourself, you may hear a voice that tells you to leave or quit or forget. You may hear your own heart telling you that you have gone off-track. You may hear a voice so clear and crisp, so loud and so close, that there is no doubting it any more. A reminder or memory so certain that you can't not explore it. So, you get busy having another baby or getting the next job or doing a renovation or trying to find 'Old Celine' loafers online because all of these things will soothe and distract you, convince you that you're fine and how that voice, that gut feeling, or 'knowing', or whatever you want to call, is full of shit anyway and doesn't know everything, and wasn't it her who told you that 'HE' was 'the one' when you were 17 and look how that ended? You can't trust her; you can't trust anyone.

Except she is *you* and she's the only voice that really matters . . . and the truth is, you know that. Everyone knows. Inside, deep down and sometimes just below the surface, you know. You know what you need, you know when you've been accepting treatment you shouldn't, you know when you've built yourself a dazzling prison, you know when you've given up or abandoned yourself. You can convince yourself that you don't have a clue, that life is happening to you and you're just breezing along as a passive passenger, but you also know that's horseshit.

The hardest thing is listening to a gentle voice within when you have spent forever drowning it out. You do not need to be fixed, to sort yourself out or to change your ways (maybe a bit!). You need to *forget* what you have learned and return home to yourself. *That* is your only job. And, once you lean into it, you will start to discover parts of yourself that are actually a bit fabulous, parts of yourself that have been buried in the rubble of your gorgeous little ego. You will start to tap into a joy that you may have forgotten was yours to begin with. It's there, I promise. Digging might sound daunting but once you get a whiff of treasure there will be no stopping you. And there *is* treasure; there's a shit tonne of gold and emeralds and all kinds of magnificent stuff hiding there. Go digging!

Perfect

When we land earthside, or 'pop out', as my daughter says with a smile my old stitches resent, we are whole, unique little beings. We are *perfect*.

Perfect /'pəːfɪkt/ adjective
having all the required or desirable elements,
qualities, or characteristics;
as good as it is possible to be.

Our hearts are fully open and we are gloriously loveable. 'As good as it is possible to be'. We are pure love. The reason babies are so beautifully enthralling is because of their whole, open hearts, not, as Michael Caine said, because they blink fewer times per minute*, although that's also pretty cute. *There's a chance I dreamt Michael Caine said this but I refuse to believe it's not true.

We love them wholly and completely. We love them when they're grumpy and shouty and needy. We love them when their faces are crumpled and they fart into our hands. Babies are demanding and uncompromising, they are tiny little divas ... they implicitly know their worth and we respond to that by giving them whatever they want at whatever ungodly hour they want it. And we give it to them with a bleary-eyed grin because they are deserving. They are pure, magnetic, wide open and that is their magic. That is also *your* magic!

As we grow up (actually pretty quickly), we begin to learn that this pure love isn't straightforward, and may even leave us at risk. The inherent openness that is the true source of our power is identified as a weakness or begins to feel too painful to maintain. The fear of loss, the vulnerability that comes with unedited love, feels risky. Bit by bit, through experience or observation or trauma, we learn to tighten just a little. To close our hearts and change our shape and fit the mould. We forget how to trust ourselves and be ourselves because we're told that being someone/something else is better/safer/more loveable.

Obviously as kids we need to be 'socialised', taught how to behave in civil society (whatever that is); what that looks like is largely up to the adults in our lives: 'You can roar like a wildling and pretend to be a lion but only when I've got the headspace for that'; 'Rough and tumble is fine as long as I say so. When we go to Granny's just be quiet. Throwing snot at your teacher is "not good" even if David Walliams thinks it's funny!' The grown-ups are making the rules up as they go along and as kids we have to bend and shift to fit those ever-changing moods and ideas.

Since our beliefs and attitudes are learned and pro-grammed when we're kids, we carry the beliefs and attitudes of the people we were surrounded by until we decide to unlearn them and choose a better way (or not). Kids know who they are until they're told who they are isn't who they should be. Our job isn't to bury the vulnerability of the child within; it's to rediscover it and love it back to life.

Who Are You?

So, who are you? Big old question. WHO ARE YOU? It sometimes feels like an assault to be asked such a direct and deeply probing question, almost aggressive.

Me? I am one of four girls. Blessed is he among women. I often open with this as if it's my most notable attribute. 'Second from the top!' Like the Spice Girls, we were gifted identities early on: the brainy one, the dancer, the tomboy, the chef! Mixed old bag, to be fair, and not as catchy as Posh or Sporty; also three Gingers made it confusing but what can you do?

We were often described as being very different from each other – shocking, considering we are individual humans – but this seemed to be quite novel, remarkable almost, maybe because we all looked so similar. Although perhaps not immediately obvious to others, our differences were wildly threatening, at least to each other. We were incredibly close, thick as thieves but we were also scrambling quite a bit – for attention, recognition, a sense of self. I say 'we', this may have been my unique experience. We were the 'girls' plural . . . that should have felt comforting in the collective and it sometimes did but I struggled, I guess like a football team if they were all just footballers – no strikers, no goalie, no defenders – just a bunch of bodies in a field not quite sure in which direction they should be going or if anyone is even watching. That sense of being a bit lost followed me.

I didn't realise how deeply this blanket reference to us had affected me. I would be asked, 'what are you into', 'what do you like to watch', and it felt like a trick – I don't bloody know! It was as if people knew that I was faking and they wanted to catch me out. It was a question I felt ill-equipped to answer but I was the only one who could answer.

My agency do this thing once a year where you all sit in a room around a big table and they present a plan for you. A big image of you – 'brand Angela' . . . 'here's what the future looks like for you, babe'. I remember sitting there one day surrounded by these brilliant and passionate brains. PowerPoint over, they all turned to me expectantly. It wasn't me. It was someone else. I didn't recognise the person they saw when they looked at me. I cried, obviously. I love a good weep, especially in an office setting.

They asked who I was? Who I wanted to be? I deflected with humour and hoped they would move on. They didn't. To be fair, it's a pretty profound question – 'who are you?' – so maybe it's not surprising that I cried but it also felt oddly unsettling to me. I was mid-thirties being asked once again 'what are you into' and finding myself caught short. No further along. I had the job, I had the potential, but my foundations were built on quicksand. Built on being told what I was and wasn't. If I was good or I wasn't. I was forever looking outside, rather than within, for validation. It never occurred to me that my unease stemmed from the fact that I was living with a stranger – myself (a flatmate I never really got to know; we shared oat milk but never secrets).

Pink Panther

I started young, creating versions of myself to suit the room. Changing to fit in and feel accepted, never quite trusting my own inner voice. I was six years old when my Uncle Johnny (the funny, suave one who lived in London and wore three-piece suits for breakfast) came to Trabolgan (like Center Parcs but in eighties Ireland). Trabolgan was where our favourite family holiday *ever* was. Not in some fancy foreign hotel with an infinity pool, or Disney World; it was in a caravan park in Co Cork. We piled into a van (this could be a slightly exaggerated re-enactment, but I swear I remember there being a van) and spent a joyous, feral week 'off grid' before anyone was really on it.

Johnny arrived with my Auntie Kathleen and two cousins. This was divine. It was exciting and I always felt drawn to them. They had left. They felt exotic. Kathleen was always impeccably dressed and drank only champagne! She would task us with giving her a 'facial', which consisted of us putting a towel-headband on her and rubbing cream on her forehead and cheeks, someone would massage her hands; sometimes she snored. I didn't even know what a facial was but I knew I wanted a life where someone rubbed my forehead while I had a snooze.

One evening, Johnny took us all to the shop on site. It was a typical holiday supermarket – milk and bread, wellies, booze, buckets and spades. It was heaven. He told us to pick one thing each. Anything. My sisters and cousins trawled the shop – *was a bike too much? . . . Yes, don't take the piss* – and everyone chose something; something they loved, something to remember, a proper treat, a souvenir. I loved Johnny; as a skinny kid he used to call me 'muscles' and make me flex my biceps. It made me laugh. I wanted more than anything for him to love me and think I was special. I decided that I would choose something . . . small.

I walked the aisles with trepidation, weighing up my options. I didn't allow myself to really think about getting something I loved or felt excited by. I had decided that if I asked for less, if I was less demanding, less grabby or needy, I was more loveable. I chose a Pink Panther bar that cost 5p. It was an E-number-filled small, strawberry-flavoured, pink chocolate bar that was absolutely delicious on a normal day but tasted of nothing that evening.

The certainty I had that my small request would be greeted with applause and appreciation evaporated almost immediately. I thought I would be publicly praised for being so lo-fi. I would be popped on a little pedestal and called a 'good girl'. But he just asked if I was sure that's all I wanted. Inside I was hoping he would say I was too fabulous and that I needed something that was just as sparkly as I was but he had six shouting kids with mounds of plastic crap and if I wanted a Pink Panther bar who was he to refuse me? So he accepted my request, beeped it through with the rest of the stuff and off we all went.

In the hope that I would somehow be identified as the best kid, the most good kid, the least grabby kid, I had deprived myself of the experience of being *just* a kid. To accept a present felt risky, like a missed opportunity to prove myself. But what I was proving was that those little desires within me could be ignored, squashed. Under the glare of the shop lights I could deny my needs and wants in the hope that somehow not needing or wanting anything made people want and need.

But the message to my six-year-old self was ask for less, need less, be *less* and you will get more of the things you want that can't be wrapped neatly in plastic and scanned at a till. You will get more love and adoration and attention. Except I didn't. I lost on both fronts. But, in my tiny,

beautiful, and fragile mind, it confirmed the secret feeling
that I was hoping might be wrong, I am worth no more
than a 5p Pink Panther bar. Nothing I could have chosen or
eaten that day would have filled me up.

Don't Look At Yourself, Look For Yourself

To discover your authentic self, to truly understand yourself, you have to start to remember who you were before you started pretending to be someone else. Who were you when you were fresh out of the oven, before parents or siblings or society started to shape you? When you were unselfconscious, uninhibited, and completely in love with yourself. Completely worthy.

When I first started to wander back and rediscover who I was – the kid version of me, which is obviously still very much a part of the adult me – I was surprised by who I found. I had ideas of myself as this glorious little beam of light, a divine laid-back baby who glided in, carefree, on glittered skates, cool and funny and ready to deliver the LOLs. I was the joker, the one who would ask silly questions to diffuse weird tension or make a tit of myself to ease someone else's discomfort. I was the welcoming committee, the caterer, and the entertainer. Or at least that was what I told myself.

The reality, when I started to revisit my childhood through memories and feelings or talking to family, was very different and the stories that kept coming up made me feel weak and embarrassed. I was a deeply sensitive child and many of the moments that really touched me and formed me didn't gel with the image I had of myself as a joyful little firecracker. I had rejected the parts of myself that were vulnerable, scared and needy, and learned to value the version of me that was feisty, jazzy and independent. In my mind I was stuck in the middle of everything, buoyant and smiling; in reality I was very often on the edge. That fear of being on the edge forever became my greatest driving force.

As children we are gloriously unapologetic about being ourselves. We revel in our unique weirdness and as a result we are completely and utterly magnetic. It's impossible to look at a kid who is whole and authentic and not fall in love; the madness and quirks, the strops and oddities all wonderfully compelling. Maybe we respect it because we wish we still had it. *The beautiful truth of who we are.* As we get older and begin to refine ourselves to suit the tastes of randomers we don't even care about, we forget who we are, and the act of being 'authentic' (the thing that we are born with, that we are given ...) now feels like something we must construct.

I realised early on that 'being yourself' was considered an act of pure rebellion rather than a natural step. In a way, that was the main appeal. Not the truth or freedom that 'being yourself' brings but the fact that it felt like a defiant thing to do. I have held on fiercely to that defiance and encouraged it in others too. Like I was defending myself from some sort of imminent attack, an attempt to wash me down and tidy my hair and spit me out like all the rest. The irony was that my commitment to unapologetically 'being me' wasn't altogether authentic! I was committed to a version of myself, committed to doing the opposite, showing up as someone completely comfortable in her own skin when the reality was very different.

I'm a red-head, and it made me 'other' as a kid and teen; I guarded it fiercely but I also resented it. I played at 'loving myself' but it was fiercely conditional and those conditions changed like the wind. As a young child it was novel; we got attention wherever we went – a little bunch of reddish heads out en masse. We were cute. Then as I got older it became a kind of quiet, unspoken shame I couldn't shake. I silently hated how different it made me. I resented how I stood out when I wanted to fit in. Lads in school would chat about girls they liked – whether they were into 'blondes or brunettes' (like they had a choice!); as a red-head I was not even in the room. So I accepted pretty early on that red-heads were not on 'the list', that I was an outside bet. This was reinforced over the years when people would tell me I was the first red-head they'd ever kissed like it was some sort of wild tick-box exercise or a secret fetish. What I heard was that I was lucky. This was further reinforced by my handsome older boyfriend who gently told me one night that I wasn't 'typically good-looking', that the lads didn't really 'get it', or get me. I was an acquired taste. It was delivered as a compliment but served as a beautifully brutal reminder to me that, once again, I was lucky to be chosen.

I wasn't conscious at the time at all but my hair became a way for me to stand out but also to shut down. It was my protection. I believed I was at once special and invisible, which is quite a heady and confusing mix for a teenager. I held on to it like a comfort blanket, defended it viciously, adored it outwardly. I was unique. But inside that very uniqueness I felt alien and alone.

Over the years I became nifty at adapting myself (my hair curiously stayed the same); maybe the performer in me made it easy. I could pop on a different mask or hat, bob and weave my way around a conversation, commit to nothing, dance with truths and untruths, agree with everything and nothing. I thought it was a skill; I would leave meetings and social events feeling even a little proud at what I had managed to achieve, how I had managed to fit in and make 'them' love me. But the further I walked away from that performance, the more I knew I had left a bit of my soul there too. In pleasing everyone (or at least that was the intention), I was selling myself and my integrity. I didn't know it but a little bit of me was being sacrificed every time I stepped away from who I really was.

"True happiness is when what you think, what you say and what you do are the same thing"

Gandhi

Authentic

Often those things are completely at odds and we don't even realise. How we show up in the world, the many faces we present, the things we say and maybe more importantly the things we don't say in order to fit in rather than rock the boat. Think about the people you're most drawn to, the ones you trust deeply; it's quite intangible but generally they are people whose thoughts, opinions and actions line up. There's a truth to them that's hard to put your finger on but you know. There's an honesty and realness to how they approach everything; they back themselves and, even if you don't always agree with everything they do, you admire their commitment to themselves and their own truth. You know where you stand and that boldness feels so free. And we could all do with a bit more freedom ...

You were born whole and ready to go. Your only job now is to unlearn all the bullshit you picked up along the way and get back to being yourself. Make it a priority to discover who you are again and to hold onto that. Talk to family, take time to go back in your mind to those stand-out memories and explore who you were. You can begin to really question what you like and what you don't like. Start small. There's a chance you've spent decades bending and shifting to others' whims; it'll take a little bit of time to hear your own voice again. Break it down and commit to being defiantly, unapologetically YOU. There is only one you.

*

Romancing Yourself

Before you hook up with someone, or at least before you settle with someone, you will get to know them, right? It's the wine-and-dine phase and no one in their right mind would skip that bit. You have thoughtful dates, you listen intently, you learn about everything they love and hate, what they were like as a kid, you explore them, you want to discover every part of them, you might even think their crap jokes are funny (at the very least, you excuse them). You are wildly eager to learn about your partner's vulnerabilities – that ritual of sharing – all aspects, all thoughts – is actually what creates deep connection. Somebody accepting you regardless of your 'weaknesses', holding you and seeing you and loving you because of – not in spite of – them; *that* is the power and wonder of falling in love.

We naturally do this mating dance with someone else or multiple people over the course of a lifetime but rarely do we give ourselves the same privilege. Now, 'romancing' yourself may feel like a stretch but could you at least spend a bit of time flirting with yourself? Figuring out your buttons, so to speak!

Sitting in silence with you and only you can feel like a gross and unimaginable thing when you've spent a lifetime running away and drowning out your own voice ... distracting with TV and books, phone calls, phone scrolls, toast, thinking about toast but refusing to have toast, work and wine. Whatever your chosen form of distraction, it doesn't really matter, you just need to be able to recognise when you begin to manically escape yourself and come back home.

When you are in love, you are drawn to all aspects of a person. You have opened your heart and are able to give yourself without fear, you drop your judgement, you are looking with fresh eyes. It's intoxicating; it drives you mental but you feel so alive. It feels like the world has changed overnight because truthfully your view of it has, and that's everything.

Now, obviously this feeling doesn't last forever and no one person can make you feel whole and happy for very long if you don't have the capacity to feel these things alone. But if you can make yourself a safe haven knowing that regardless of what's going on around that you can always come home then you can stay open for the good stuff safe in the knowledge that you can survive the bad. That's the payoff. And it's something I must still remind myself about.

There is no one-size-fits-all and that should be obvious – we all like different things, we are different beings. What makes one person swoon will make you cringe, that's OK! Check in, ask questions, listen intently, keep in touch – with yourself. When you are disconnected, you're kind of flying blind, but if you can come back to yourself regularly, take yourself out, you are less likely to fly too far from your centre.

Make yourself a refuge. Make yourself the one you want to hang out with. The one you can turn to, depend and rely on. Spend time properly getting to know yourself. Your inner state reflects your experience of the outside world. If you love yourself fully and compassionately, you will experience the world through that lens. If you offer yourself compassion, you will offer it to everyone you encounter. If you really love yourself, you will begin to love people without condition – like you're falling in love every day ... not with the hot one from Starbucks but with life.

*

Hide and Seeking

Getting to know yourself on a deep level means getting familiar with parts of yourself you've eaten! The parts of yourself that, for whatever reason, feel less acceptable – to you and others. The hard thing is you'll be discovering these parts forever. The AMAZING thing is you'll be discovering these things forever!

Here's some truth. I had an eating disorder for 15 years. Anorexia and bulimia. Even writing that feels terrifying. Shoving it out there under your nose, no Tipp-Ex (retro reference), no denial. I denied it for years, of course, to my friends and family, to myself. I denied it to everyone. It was disgusting or I was superior. It was never an issue that needed tender handling; it was a choice I made that was annoying and stubborn and inconvenient for everyone involved, most of all me.

I never took it seriously even with hindsight and distance and enough confidence to believe it's history. I balk slightly at the notion that I had an 'ED'. I am in 'recovery' ... am I? Does that even apply to me?

I never took it seriously because I didn't fall over. I never took it seriously even when I fell over. In a way it wasn't to be feared, it wasn't my enemy it was my closest friend, the one who really knew me, who knew my pain and could help me escape it rather than feel it. It was my master too. A punishing, unrelenting master who pushed me further and further away from myself. Who delighted in my world closing in, and enjoyed my agonising loneliness, although it was neatly dressed as independence.

I used to look at this period of my life with tremendous sadness. I was ashamed. I knew intellectually that this was my 'chosen' coping mechanism. I wished I was strong enough to just cope without a mechanism. I think I wished that I was a machine, made up of mechanisms that allowed me to operate without limits. I was embarrassed by my over-sensitivity, annoyed at my seeming inability to just deal with the bigness of life (a good life!) and all the hideously messy feelings it brings. I swallowed them instead. I stopped trusting myself and my feelings, believing somehow that I was just a bit soft and that life required me to 'toughen up'. I felt out of control, like I was born without the right equipment to survive this world. My eating disorder gave me something I could control, all day, every day. It seduced me into believing it was me who held the wheel.

One issue, among many others, with an eating disorder is the sheer sense of isolation that comes along with it. So many of the activities, the everyday events, the social habits and rituals that serve to enrich our lives are tied to food; where there should be joy, there is only angst. An alcoholic can remove booze from their surroundings and avoid situations where it's present; it's not easy but it's clear-cut. If your addiction of choice is food (restricting or bingeing/purging), you cannot just give up or avoid food, at least not forever. So, in recovery, every single seemingly simple daily interaction is a challenge. An obstacle to be overcome. Like doing a pub crawl on your first dry week.

On top of that is the pressure and anger that comes from a lack of understanding around eating disorders. It can be hard to fully enjoy yourself if it's clear your tablemate is not, as if their restriction and discomfort ruins your experience. The person with the eating disorder becomes somehow responsible, an unintentional doubling down. An extra pinch of shame. And that shame seasons everything. It stays in your system long after dinner. For me, saying it out loud punches a hole in the shame. Owning it feels like a compassionate thing to do. The pretending, the distance, the denial was like the ultimate rejection of the bit of me that couldn't cope, punishing the me that was just trying to make me feel safe. Giving it air, naming it and examining it made it less powerful and gave me validation and relief. It allowed me to see the eating disorder as a thing I did, not who I was. 'It' was something; 'it' was not the whole of me. And in knowing it and owning 'it', I stole its power and took back my own.

Not-So Lovely Lady Lumps

Caroline taught me. I mean, not in the way an actual teacher teaches you things. But I heard her talking – selling it in the school toilets one day. 'You basically eat everything, chuck it up and start again tomorrow.' Sounded simple. And exotic, which seems bizarre now because the whole thing is hideous but in that moment she was glorious and this other world seemed oddly fascinating and more appealing than the one I existed in.

Caroline was always more grown-up, right from the start. Her uniform fit her, none of the gangly teenage limbs. She was squat and child-beary. She looked ripe. Not perfect, that wasn't her appeal. Her face, like her body, was a bit squashed too, which I imagined made boys imagine themselves beneath her, also squashed. My clothes were always too big; my hips, like a prepubescent boy. I wanted lumps. Filthy lumps stuffed with cellulite-proof of womanhood. I was tiny. Dwarfed. 'Good goods come in small parcels.' That's what she said. Not Caroline. My mam. I cringed as I heard myself say it out loud. Small parcels, fuck sake.

Buying my first bra was a family event; my 'buds' had popped and they needed sorting. We all laughed. I died a little. 28AA. What was the point? Cheeks reddened. Buds flattened. I kept them down. I ran for days and kept them at bay. Overnight they grew. Full blown. 'Did she get a boob job?' I didn't. I wanted to disappear them, to invisible them. Eyes were on them. Eyes on me. I strapped them down. Those Shakira mounds – neither small nor humble . . . intruders.

Of course, Caroline had tits before the rest of us. Maybe because her loins were awake, the other woman bits of her knew she was ready and she seemed fine with it. I would never be ready. It felt like I was being forced to enter a stage against my will. Run before I could walk. My period didn't come for years. I watched them buckled over, aching but victorious. A club I didn't have a wristband for. But I danced competitively, and much like a gymnast I figured things were stunted. Under control. That felt safer even if I wasn't part of the crew. There was power in me stopping time. Keeping womanhood at arm's-length.

Some girls are born to be women. Like Jessica Rabbit, Cardi B, Beyoncé. They have a power that is intoxicating. Tomboys were invisible. Mucky, but not in the sexy way. Being a proper woman was not appealing to me. The power, the strength, the sheer divinity of the woman, the source of all creation was lost on me then. To be a woman meant to be overlooked, weak. It meant doing all the work but getting none of the glory. It meant washing up. Picking up. Holding up. Everyone but yourself.

Womanhood meant sacrifice and denial. Denial of need and desire. It meant surrendering your dreams and ambitions and finding a man who could pay for things so you didn't have to. To be a woman meant to shrink. Literally and otherwise. To dim and hide so as not to draw undue attention. Do not take up room or air or light. Stay quiet, stay small. Know. Your. Place.

Fuck that.

So I rejected any signs of femininity. I strapped down my breasts with double sports bras, I hardened; my energy was aggressive, competitive. I would make sure that I was considered an equal. I would show just how much I could keep up and show up. I would abandon all of the wonderful, quiet, knowing power that comes with embodying the divine feminine. I would strive to be 'one of the lads.' A win for us as a collective but a severing of the cord that kept me tethered to myself.

The Cure

I 'cured' myself of my eating disorder very quickly, very conveniently and seemingly overnight. I'm an overachiever like that and the rules that apply to most don't apply to me. Or at least that's what I told myself. The idea that I would have to dig and trudge through some childhood bullshit was tedious to me. I didn't have time for any of that; I had an empire to build. My addiction and escape into food was neatly replaced by an addiction to work. The relentless commitment, obsession, devotion I once reserved for food was now turned to my career.

I was insatiable, indefatigable, persistent, and enthusiastic. Some people might say I was hungry. In fact I was fucking starving. Not literally, of course – remember I was 'cured' – but I was desperate to succeed; it was like my life depended on it.

For a long time my identity was my eating disorder; now it shifted, overnight, to my job. It's worth noting that I had no idea I had made this switch, so quietly commanding and manipulative is that voice. I genuinely believed I had fixed myself. I had 'snapped' out of it. A dramatic break-up and the realisation that I would now have to pave my own path, rather than accompany someone else down theirs, focused my mind.

I read an article that told me that a binge/purge episode took fourteen days to 'get over', two whole weeks for the body and appetite to normalise (whatever that is). I didn't have days to waste, never mind weeks. I was against the clock, scrambling to find a purpose and a place and find it quick. I often cited this as a turning point. But truthfully I think the turning point came earlier, or at least the planting of the seed that would grow into a quiet determination to break out of the tiny little prison I lived in. It took me years to crawl towards that place, away from the cage. I didn't want to be a statistic. I did not want my heart to stop like Karen Carpenter. I did not want to die. I wanted to win. That was my motivation above all else. To 'beat it'. It was not an act of self-love; it took me much longer to get there.

So back at work, around the clock, a new woman. I was feeling smug about my miraculous transformation. A friend once joked that she wished she had picked work as her chosen addiction and to be fair I felt a bit relieved that it was now mine. It afforded me a beautiful life, security and travel, brilliant and bizarre experiences. It had even made me a bit special; certainly, I became more interesting the more people saw me on TV, in magazines. There were upsides for sure. But the downside was that no one tried to stop me. Of course, I could have stopped myself; except I couldn't. Like a binge with no end in sight. To all who could see, I was thriving. I didn't run out of cash or collapse in a gutter, my skin looked fresh; there was no need for an intervention. My 'rock bottom' was very hard to identify; arguably my 'rise' coincided with my descent. The harder I worked, the higher I climbed, the more I was cheered from the sidelines. It was like some cruel nightmare. Instead of helping me, people praised me for my fantastic work ethic. Conversations centred around what was next, could I do more: 'you only get one shot', 'there are a million people who would kill to be in your position', 'make hay while the sun shines'. I made hay. I made all the fucking hay until I wanted to crawl underneath it and set it alight.

I tell you all this not so that you too can give me a round of applause (although I'll never turn that down). I tell you because I spent a long and lonely time denying myself any joy in life. Punishing myself, sacrificing relationships (and actual chips) and convincing myself that if I was successful enough or thin enough that I would then *be* enough. Until I committed to real change, I would just be swapping out one identify for another – a dramatic makeover for the benefit of everyone but myself. And while real change requires deeper commitment – excavation that feels painful and tedious and relentless – there is also something kind of thrilling in knowing that your way of being isn't working but that there is ANOTHER way. You can start again and rewire, you can choose for things to happen in a different way rather than just hitting the default button. You can decide through desperate snotty sobs to reach for something better.

Self-knowledge then is the beginning of a glorious new journey. It allows you to feel empowered and hopeful about the direction of your life. To fully understand yourself in all your wild complexity. Accepting the madness and unpredictability means you're in the driving seat, no longer being controlled by the three-year-old you! To reconnect with your inner child and get to know her on a deep level means you become capable of parenting yourself, you soften to yourself, and that connection reminds you that joy is within reach, and it is yours for the taking.

You are enough.

Even if you feel it in your bones that somehow you are wrong or off or not quite right, you are perfect. You are worthy of more love than you could ever need. You are deserving of everything you desire.

Chapter Two

Joyriding

> "To reach for joy in a world determined to make you live in fear is an act of anarchy"

Me!

Let's Talk About Joy, Baby

The idea of allowing joy into my life a few years ago seemed laughable. It was so far from where I was and felt like a ridiculously childish thing to hope for. Like joy was something you grow out of – life gets serious, there's stuff to do, and the freedom of adulthood comes with a cost. That cost for me was joy. I assumed it was the same for everyone else. Joy is the thing that was missing from my life and it had been missing for so long that I wasn't even sure what it would look like if I saw it; I just knew I wanted a sniff of it! However unachievable it felt, I was determined to chase it down. And I have been seeking it out ever since. That doesn't mean that I am blindly unaware of the horrors that exist in the world or that I choose to ignore the hard stuff in pursuit of some idyllic fairy tale, but I prioritise joy and I try to inject it into everyday life, even if it's just a nugget: a bracing dip that reminds me I'm alive; a call with a friend who thinks I'm funny or makes me wee with laughter (both equally rewarding); a ridiculously colourful outfit; bingeing a new series or re-watching an old favourite; eating Turkish

Delight in bed. I began to write lists of the tiny little everyday things that inject a bit of joy into my life for the days or
weeks when I forget how to find that. Something I could go
back to when things felt heavy, to remind myself that it is
possible ... There's a list at the end of this book with space
for you to add your own when they come to you.

Wtf is Joy Anyway?

It's not naive or innocent; to strive for a life filled with joy is wild. It is child-like and lion-hearted. It is hopeful, which sounds great except that hope makes us tender. Joy is not gifted, it is earned. It is only available to those who are courageous enough to sit in the pain. Those who will – however tentatively – explore their depths. Root around in the shadows to discover aspects of themselves they'd long forgotten or aspects they wish they could ignore. Only by wrapping a loving arm around the shoulder of your shadows and guiding them into the light can you stand to bask in real joy.

But what the hell is joy really? Some elusive Hallmark illusion? There are such expectations around it. We should feel it, we should experience it daily, hourly ... but what does it *feel* like anyway? What does it look like? Christmas? Is there a whiff of cinnamon and stuffing in the air, the promise of gifts and gin and maybe a lie-in if you're lucky ...? 'Joy to the world, the Lord has come!'

Joy is different for everyone; it comes dressed in an array of glittering outfits or a comfy grey tracksuit. Joy is everywhere but it is our job to defiantly chase it down and allow it into our lives. To stay open enough to let it in every day. I'm not talking about 'toxic joy'; this is not empty flaunting or hollow displays of happiness for the benefit of strangers. It isn't loud or attention-seeking. The joy you're longing for is the quiet kind. It is a glow; an ember in the pit of your stomach. It is a soft breeze or a belly laugh. It is the warmth you feel when you watch a child sleeping or the peace you feel when you wake from a bad dream to a sweaty shoulder that feels like home. It is presence. Knowing what you have before it is gone. Because it will be. It will ebb and flow and come and go. Like a bird, you can't hold onto it, but you can fly alongside.

Sounds ideal! But you have to be open to feeling that ... fully open, blown wide open, and that is bloody terrifying. It is intense to lean headlong into joy. It is intensely vulnerable to fully feel the weight of love knowing that it may not always be this way. Being fearless in embracing joy and intimacy, when it's there, can feel immense. It can be difficult to receive those feelings and acknowledge those perfect little moments in time because, in acknowledging them fully, you bring your awareness to their transience. Things don't last. Feelings aren't forever. People aren't forever.

Don't taint these beautiful, fleeting moments with guilt or fear, don't let the past creep in or the future rob you;

be bold enough to stay right in the moment. In *this* moment. If we could apply the 'what would you do if it was your last day on earth?' mentality to every day that we're lucky enough to wake up to, we would live with such ferocity that being extinguished wouldn't even matter. We would live so fiercely and fearlessly that regret would never weigh on us. Fear would never stop us from doing what we want, from prioritising who we love and thriving unapologetically. We would be free to stop living our lives by other people's rules and start making our own. If you're ready for that, let's crack on!

Maybe for you joy has been ever-present in your life, an easy reach. Maybe you're so busy doing life that you assume you don't have time for that nonsense. It is idealistic bullshit. Maybe, like me, you need a jolt; something so big it shakes you to the core and makes you question everything? For many people, the arrival of a baby is a purely joyful experience, the memory of that deliciously fuzzy head and the cosy baby bubble, the mad rush of emotions, time stopping, overwhelming love. The act of becoming a parent is surely the *very* definition of joy; at least that's what I imagined when I looked around at everyone else. My own experience was somewhat different, but it was also the start of something magic.

Here's the truth: when I had my daughter, my world turned upside down. Every feeling, every fear I had escaped or plastered over or run from forever, confronted me in the form of this tiny human who needed me more than anything in the world. I was a mother. I was supposed to know what I was doing. I was supposed to be engulfed by this overwhelming sense of love, to exist in a bubble with this beautiful little soul, but instead I was shit. I had no idea what I was doing, which now seems like an obvious experience (NO ONE KNOWS), but at the time I felt like a complete failure. I was scared, my nipples were sore, I was falling apart. I looked at my daughter one day while on a very clipped maternity leave and realised that we were both lost little souls floating together without a clue. I had been given a gift; she had been gifted a dud.

My chapped nipples and aching back were a grim metaphor for my inadequacy. I felt sorry for her and the realisation of that almost broke me – it was such an admission of defeat, such a disloyal, cruel thought. It was also infuriating. I have always been good at stuff. A competent human. An overachiever. I got things done. I was deliciously competitive and usually won. I was not a loser. I was not supposed to be drowning. I was not supposed to be desperate. But I was.

I have had anxiety and depression; I have had an eating disorder and post-natal . . . *something*. Was it mania, or was it a breakdown of sorts? I'm not quite sure. All I know is that I have lived for many years split in two: my outside face beaming and smiling, relentlessly positive; inside in turmoil. I would put my mask on and do the thing, then come home and crawl back into a shell that felt like a foreign country. I felt like the two versions were me, but one was acceptable, and one wasn't. One was love-able and one wasn't. One was tolerable and one was repulsive.

At eighteen months, my daughter taught me one of my greatest lessons. She toddled into our bedroom one morning and made her way to the floor-length mirror. She looked in the mirror and checked herself out: not in the way that I would – making sure my arse isn't hanging out or checking the proportions of an outfit that worked in my head but hadn't been road-tested. Instead, she actually looked at herself, *into* herself, and it knocked me sideways. She was deeply, madly, purely in love with her reflection and I felt a pang of jealousy.

This foreign scene unfolding before me jarred so hard it made me realise that not only did I not 'love' myself, or even like myself, I hardly *knew* myself. That day, I made a commitment to wake up and fall back in love with myself. To treat the toddler me with the same compassion and patience and love I gave my daughter without question. This love hadn't been earned – she didn't 'give' me anything (in fact, all she did was take – attention, milk, sleep, my husband's heart!) – but her wholeness was everything. It was time to get mine back …

'Your joy will come,' says the universe. 'So will your love, of course. But first I must show you yourself – your actions and thoughts – again and again, in the mirrors of your own life. You must come deeply to terms with yourself and know and understand your many wild and hidden parts, not simply for what they are but for what they will show you. Then you will hold them to the light, gently letting go of what must leave. You will come to know more, and understand that you know even less. This is the very beginning"

Yrsa Daley-Ward

Gravitating Towards Gratitude

In a state of desperation, I consumed podcasts around the clock, eating books to help me find some sanity and buying face masks and all manner of shit that promised to lift me up! I started to mainline 'gratitude', remembering *The Secret* and other books I read in my twenties and how it had turned my life around. I started a podcast 'Thanks A Million' on that very subject, not because I'm some guru on gratitude but because I desperately needed to commit to it and figured if I bought equipment and launched a thing (for work) I might stick to it, for once.

According to Oprah Winfrey, who is the oracle on all things, 'If you look at what you have in life, you'll always have more. If you look at what you don't have in life, you'll never have enough.' She's good, in fairness, but I'd heard it all before; I believed it but actually living it is much tricker than posting it online.

Practising gratitude is not some fluffy new-age bull-shit. It's not a dusty quote hanging in the changing room of a regional boutique. It is now one of the most widely recognised methods for improving your overall well-being but like with many tried-and-tested methods it can be easily overlooked. Much like being told that the key to physical health is to move more, eat whole, we don't always want to hear it. Sometimes we just want to eat and chill, sometimes we just want to wallow or swallow a pill. But sometimes we owe it to ourselves to push through, take matters into our own hands and give ourselves a little bit more of what's good for us.

And the practice of gratitude, it turns out, was good for me. It is virtually impossible to feel fear or sadness while feeling grateful at the same time. Being grateful impacts the overall experience of happiness, and the effects tend to be long-lasting. It's also free and quick and easy, which is why, ironically, I took it for granted for so long. Hand me something shinier, newer, more expensive. Give me the fad or a quick fix NOW. I don't want slow and steady; I want a delicious wallop of instant gratification. I don't want 'work'; I want an easy win. The idea of consistent application of anything felt dull to me, like a nine-to-five. I imagined it might kill me or at the very least render me robotic. But it turns out that routine does indeed 'set you free'! Or perhaps it sets you up to grow – routines allow space for habits to form (good ones) and habitual application of positive habits changes the mind, how you feel about yourself and how your life unfolds as a result.

What's the first thing you do in the morning after you wake? Grab your phone. Scroll. Remember an old friend's birthday. Get shocked by another human tragedy. Notice an ex got a new job. A peer living her best life. Rinse and repeat. You wake and jump back into a cycle. Feeling the same feeling, identifying as the same self, repeating old, familiar patterns. It feels a bit underwhelming (or maybe overwhelming), compression in your chest, a resigned sigh – but it's familiar, and familiar is safe, even if it's a bit crap. You talk yourself out of bed, hop in the shower on autopilot, brush your teeth, have the usual breakfast. You are basically freewheeling. Your mind and body don't have to think; all these actions are automatic, based on everything you've ever done in the past. They (your mind and body) learn to do all the stuff you do daily with little thought or effort, freeing you up to be creative, giving you space and conserving energy. But the reality is every day you freewheel you are thrown back into the past. You are living Groundhog Day but without the genius and humour Bill Murray brings. You are stuck in a loop – same feeling, same experience, same frustration.

So, we need to get conscious about how we show up every day. 'Show up' – that's very American, isn't it? But it matters. We 'show up' to meetings, dates and parties, we get togged out, made up and in the zone, for other people mostly, which is nice, but how often do you 'show up' for yourself? If we want to live a fuller, more deliberate life then we need to decide to wake, get out the other side of the bed and actively choose a different path, choose to look at life through a different lens.

Your only job is to follow joy. That might sound heady and unrealistic when you're stuck in traffic, you've been up all night with screaming kids, you're broke or you've just lost a friend. It might sound like rubbish … impossible. But the truth is that you have choices every single day, every single moment of every single day. You can place your attention on and be consumed by what is wrong, by the things that make you feel sad and stuck or less than – OR you can make a conscious choice to move your attention to something better.

I heard this for a million years: 'your only job is to follow good feelings'. Easy. Except it's not. It seems impossible – a mammoth, insurmountable task – when you're on the ground and trying to drag yourself from a dark hole. Getting dressed, brushing your teeth … even the simplest tasks may seem hard. The pursuit of 'joy' is a reach when simply feeling 'not shit' is a challenge. (The caveat here is clinical depression, of course, but generally speaking we do have choices and we can make decisions daily to improve our lives and help us emerge from the funk. We can empower ourselves.)

It is often a choice to stay stuck, just as it's a choice to take a leap into the unknown. Where you are may be bad but the fear of uncertainty can seduce you into believing it's better than what's 'out there', since you don't actually know what's out there and you cannot control it. Better to stay where you are even if it's squeezing you slowly . . .

The suggestion that you can take responsibility may feel like an assault, like an aggressive accusation. The idea that you can take responsibility for your own life can feel more like a weight than an opportunity. But let's be honest, sometimes it's easier to believe that things are happening to you and completely out of your control. You can hide or blame someone else, something else, but by choosing this supposedly safe place you're at the mercy of the world rather than creating a world that feels good for you. It takes commitment and discipline to decide to own it all – the good and the bad – but once you feel the shift you will never NOT do it.

Optimism and happiness are the results of spiritual work

Marianne Williamson, *A Return to Love*

Joyriding

Abraham Hicks calls it 'rampaging' ... a process of moving towards a 'better feeling' feeling! Following momentum, listing the positives in any situation, CHOOSING to see things in a better way and thus feeling better too. And, in feeling better, you align to a better vibration, attracting more positive things in, and having more things to be grateful for.

I call it 'joyriding': consciously swerving into a sweeter lane, noticing all the good stuff as you drive by, wind in your hair (!) luxuriating in it; choosing to love your life or at least feel OK about it in any given moment; making a choice to focus on what's working for you rather than obsessing over what isn't.

How though?? I don't need the words. Tell me what to do, I hear you shout at the back. I'm with you: I need practical examples, not platitudes. 'I am SO LUCKY.' I started saying this to myself years ago; actually my mam said it from the time we were kids, that we had been born lucky, we were lucky as 'cut cats', whatever that meant. I didn't care, it felt like a little gift, a sort of invisible superpower. I didn't feel especially lucky at this point in my life;

my state of mind meant that no matter how lucky I was on paper, I couldn't feel it at all.

I was living in a damp old flat in East London, trying to figure out how to make what felt like a monumental move work: a career change late in the game. I was strapped for cash, I was lonely, and I desperately needed to make things work, so – like any determined, bright and young-ish woman – I spent what pennies I had on some overpriced bed sheets. Stay with me. I shelled out what little I had on a decent thread count and a foamy mattress and would start the day as if I had woken up in a 5-star hotel. I figured I needed to wake up well if I wanted to step into the world in a better state. I'd set my alarm a few minutes early and in that hazy in-between instead of groaning about a mediocre sleep, rolling over or checking my phone, I began to intentionally set up my mood for the day. I would properly feel the cotton on my skin, being grateful that I could buy these sheets, that I had somewhere warm to sleep, that my body was relaxed and rested, there was heat in the house and food in the fridge. I had a sheepskin mat that my feet would touch as soon as I got out of bed. I'd feel the warm water in the shower and smell the shampoo ... 'How lucky I am to be able to buy shampoo that smells like washed puppy and pineapple!?' I would open my wardrobe and feel a rush of gratitude at all the options I had, in how many ways I could express myself (with camouflage and sequins, mostly together but that's a different story). What would I have for breakfast? 'I am so thankful to have a fridge full of eggs!' You get the gist . . . !

Focusing on all of the things I had previously taken for granted every day in favour of fixating on what someone had/did/owned/achieved down the road. No matter how seemingly insignificant or unglamorous these things might be, properly tuning into them shifts how we feel on a profound level. We feel full before we even enter the world. And the magical thing is when we approach the world from that place, more good stuff shows up: people; attitudes; coincidence; luck; JOY. Doors open, blocks clear and there is an ease and a flow that may have previously felt exclusive to a blessed few. The knowledge that you can take control and create that feeling by yourself with a little intention and attention is a game-changer.

Gratitude is the ultimate state of receivership

Dr Joe Dispenza

Enough Already

It is from the state of feeling full and whole and ENOUGH that you will attract more abundance. When you need nothing, the world is open to you. When you create a state in your mind, the subconscious doesn't know what's real and what's imagined, so if you can sit in a state of gratitude, and feel that on a deep level before it has materialised, your reality will begin to line up with this image (more on that later). You will draw to you things on that vibrational level. Now, 'vibration' might sound a bit hippie or filthy, depending on your sensibilities, but it's essentially energy. We are made of energy – our bodies, our thoughts, everything – and we attract things/people/experiences that are a similar vibration to us. Think about when you walk into a room and get a 'vibe' about someone; they might be a wonderful, inoffensive onesie-wearing human but for some unknown reason you just don't click or connect. They're operating at a different vibrational level! Some people liken it to a radio station – we're all on different frequencies, and we align with those on a similar wavelength to ourselves. But we can change, control and increase our vibration so we don't need to be stuck in the same gear all day every day.

Now ... obviously you can get up in the morning
and love your clothes and your smelly shampoo and have
some buttery scrambled eggs and feel high as a kite on life
and ready for a glorious day to unfold. You can even feel
smug in your knowledge that you have got this and the universe has got your back, as Gabby Bernstein would say,
but ... Then the train line is down and some dickhead in
the coffee shop spills his cortado on your trench coat and
doesn't even apologise, Google told you it would be sunny
but it's starting to spit and you're wearing Birkenstocks
instead of Docs. Now, you're going to be late because you've
got to take the car but you forgot your keys and is there even
enough petrol in there anyway? He never bloody fills it up
after using it, so selfish. Seriously, an hour ago you were rolling in your new sheets and thinking about how sweet life is.
Fuck this!

AND. BREATHE.

It's easy to be thankful and grateful when there is a
lot to be thankful and grateful for. Even if they are everyday
things you didn't previously notice, once you focus, there
are tangible positive benefits that you can fixate on and use
to raise your vibrations and feel better. It's tougher when
the shit hits the fan. This is when you need to properly flex
those muscles. It's not called 'a practice' for nothing. Start to
do it, challenge yourself to see the good in the worst

situations, in the worst people! Look for their soul, look for the lesson, look for the humour.

For example, consider this version of events . . . You are late for work and stuck in traffic. That swell of anxiety and frustration rises. However, neither the anxiety nor the frustration will get you to work any faster. You don't spend the journey berating yourself, willing the situation to change, thinking about everything you could have or should have done differently. Instead you *choose* a different way. You accept those frustrations and decide to change lanes. You take a 'Joyride.'

Sit in your car and make a choice to turn this 'bad' experience into a good one. The heated seat feels so good, you kind of forgot what a beautiful luxury that is. How lovely it is to have 15 minutes where you properly have nothing to do. There's nothing you can do. The radio is on. It's your favourite show – how cool is the radio!? You favourite voices and artists literally nattering to you in the car and you don't even have to make small talk. You are so lucky to have this car. To have the money to buy this car. To have a car that can take you anywhere you want to go. Imagine. You can literally go wherever you want! You are able to pick up your friends or your kids and hit the road. You have a job to go to that is teaching you and actually they're pretty understanding. You have money to go for lunch. To take a break and breathe in some fresh air. This stolen 15 minutes can be made up without major drama. Maybe it's a little gift. Surrender and say thanks for this enforced surprise time out. ENJOY IT. FEEL IT. RIDE IT! SHIFT ...

Where possible, the aim is to always shift into a better gear! I'm not saying deny the feeling or bury it, but you can recognise the feeling and reach for something even a tiny bit better. It is not possible all the time to move to a better-feeling place and there will be days when you're swimming against the tide: when everything has gone horribly wrong and it feels like you just want to crawl back into bed and wake up when it's all over or when you feel fit enough to try again. That's OK too. Sometimes the only way to get on with your day is to draw a line under it, go back to bed and get out the other side tomorrow! Thanks but no thanks, and hit the hay.

If bed is not an option and a gear shift feels out of reach in the moment, then let it hit you hard. Feel it fully; buckle under its weight and have a proper ugly cry if that's what it calls for, but give yourself a time limit. Wallow. Mill around in that misery for a bit – it may be minutes or hours – but then before it drags you down, draw a line. If you stay stuck, you will bring more of the same. The same mood or madness or discontent. A deliberate intentional change of focus will lift your mood and your perspective;

it will also change what comes into your life. You can choose your feelings but only if you're open to ALL of them.

Do not swallow your rage because it's unattractive or unacceptable. Anger, sadness, fear, frustration and the rest of the 'negative emotions' are as natural as laughter and should be welcomed without judgement. Allow them to burst into the air, or stomp them into the earth. Free your body of these emotions or they will leak out anyway. They will leak out in the way you see people; they will seep into everything you do and pop out of your mouth as passive aggression aimed at the people you love. That will offer a quick release in the moment but you will not be satisfied for long. And you will never really know where it came from. So recognise it, feel it and then move on up.

Some of the things I do to shift my energy:
Breathe deep
Have a cold shower/swim
Dance/move
Hug
Laugh – even if you have to fake it
Go for a walk in nature
Swim
Have sex

Watch a sad/happy/aggressive film

Scream into a pillow

Shout in the garden

Have crisps in the bath

Journal it out

Call a friend

Meditate

Cry

Sing

Joy Crumbs

We get one shot. We are here. YOU ARE HERE. Stop worrying about what some nameless dickhead thinks about you and let's go. Start to look at the things that you're good at and properly seek out the things that light you up. Is there a gift or talent you have that you take for granted because it's so effortless you could do it in your sleep with absolute ease? Or something you do when no one is watching that makes you feel full as a bus ... Often we overlook the things that come easiest, believing there should be a slog or a fight to succeed. That we need to work hard and struggle to be 'successful' or happy. But it doesn't all have to be an uphill battle; in fact, if it feels like one, chances are you're not doing the things you love.

Start small. Perhaps you used to enjoy painting or playing music, but your spark has faded over time; you've lost confidence or dismissed it as childish, unproductive, or unprofitable. Give in to your small desires to explore things you've abandoned and override the part of you that makes you feel like painting in the nude is pointless! If you're into it, babe, let it all hang out. The things that you chase with your heart are what will give you the most sustenance and allow you to tap into a well of joy that is not often commonplace. It feels rebellious to shut shop early and go swimming or take a day off to do some gardening; find that little rebel hidden beneath your jacket and let her out.

Obviously, most of us must make a living so just doing what you love is not a realistic 24/7 situation. Of course, if you can turn your passion into your pension then great, but not everything needs to be a side hustle. It is still worth making time and creating space in your life for the things that touch you. Your heart stuff, whatever that might be ... Allow space for things to open up, to unfold, to surprise you! No expectations.

What do you spend most of your money on (outside essentials)? What are you reading? What accounts do you scroll? These are the things to pay attention to. Not what you've been conditioned to believe is a good path or a sensible choice or an admirable route but what you would genuinely do for nothing. Is there a job you think 'yep, I'd happily do that forty hours a week with a smile, for free probably.' The jobs I know are for me are the jobs I would do without getting paid. Not that I actually work for nothing, and it doesn't mean I'm not motivated by money – I actually love it – BUT generally, if I know I'd want to do it regardless, it's a no-brainer. That is my soul shouting FUCK YES!

A 'hell yeah' is maybe better known as 'following your bliss', a term coined by Joseph Campbell, but it can sound like an option afforded to only a privileged minority. A small group who have the luxury and financial freedom to be able to do what they love, what 'lights them up' without the inconvenience of bills or rent. In reality you have a mortgage to pay or college loans hanging over you, you're starting a family or you're single and not even close to feeling financially secure. You do not have to jump ship without a boat. There is *no* rush. You are not running out of time. You do not need to do overnight what someone has spent a lifetime working towards. Equally do not give up because you assume you can't catch up.

Don't *not* do a thing because you feel someone else has got it covered. You will bring your own authentic flavour to whatever you do and there is more than enough room for all of us.

Do you love baking but you want a nice house in the suburbs so you suck it up in a city job you hate? Are you into dogs but can't envisage a world where hanging out with hounds might pay the bills? You don't have to think that far ahead. You don't need to know all of the answers or even the destination; in fact, being too absolute may mean you're blind to opportunities that are left field but even better.

You may not be able to ditch your desk job just yet (or ever) but no matter what your situation, you can start tapping into the things that make you feel alive and give you some joy. It could be on a weekend, or an evening, or when the kids are finally in bed and you get a minute to yourself. This time can be spent watching Netflix or you can unleash your inner child and start to reintroduce and rediscover the stuff you love to do. For no reason other than that it makes you feel good.

It may take a while; many of us have moved so far away from ourselves that we don't really know what we like to do. Just rediscovering that and giving it space, just KNOWING what you need to feed your soul is enough to give you relief. The knowing alone will give you some sense of peace, and honouring yourself in these small ways will fill you up.

Shout It, Sing It, Share It, Spread It

Don't underestimate the power of desire. Desire is your North Star. Of course you desire many material things and that's cool; I love nice shit . . . I really LOVE IT. But deep soul desire is different to pimping your life with delicious things you don't *really* need. Your desire will guide you to where you need to go, help you find your path and stay on it. You will never desire something you are not capable of manifesting into your life. It may take a slightly different form, show up in a different way but your desires are yours; they are clues to how your life could be.

I used to think if I trucked along quietly, out of sight, under the radar, I would be safer. If I stayed blasé about the things I longed for and never fully expressed how much I wanted to do/be/have something in my life then no one (not even me) could see when I failed. When the wish remained unfulfilled, at least I could skulk away quietly; I could feast on the failure and shame in private, alone. Somehow that would be less painful; at least no one would know. But the problem with never expressing out loud what you want is that, if it doesn't happen, you're alone (which was the plan), but if it DOES happen, you're alone too. You commiserate and celebrate on your own. Both your sorrow and joy are experienced only by you. No holding up but also no cheering.

The comfort you crave, or the elation you long to share, become solitary experiences. The disappointment isn't less but the enjoyment of a win is massively diminished. Brené Brown puts it brilliantly in *The Gifts of Imperfection*: 'I learned that playing down the exciting stuff doesn't take the pain away when it doesn't happen. It does, however, minimise the joy when it does happen.' We don't exist in isolation; our joys and sorrows are made infinitely more bearable, more memorable and more meaningful, when we let others in.

You do not have to diminish your joy to protect others. Dimming your light, shrinking yourself, giving away your power – none of these things will make you more loveable or less threatening to the right people. If you allow yourself to step away from fear and into the wholeness of who you are, you will also ignite that spark in all those you meet. You will give them permission to step into the fullness of who they are too.

Chapter Three

The Fight for Joy
(and All the Other Stuff)

Now, when we talk about 'feeling feelings', it's generally with a focus on the so-called negative ones – pain, shame, frustration, anger – encouraging us to feel safe in exploring the emotions usually thrown into the shadows. But just as we need to allow space for these feelings, we also need to fully support the good ones too. We need to give ourselves permission to feel joy and love, happiness and satisfaction too, which may sound like a no-brainer but is pretty frigging challenging at times. We are allowed to believe that these states can be reached and we can strive for more without guilt or fear.

We often hear the phrase 'it's OK not to be OK' but we rarely hear 'it's OK to *feel* OK'. Actually, it's OK to feel fucking fantastic except that most of us don't really believe that. The world has taught us that it's arrogant and naive to think we're deserving of total happiness. The world doesn't work like that. Life is hard; that's just the way it is. Shut up and put up. The idea that you might want more and believe you deserve more may be affronting to some people. It feels smug to respond to a 'how are you?' with 'I feel great/

wonderful/happy? Mostly we shift to 'fine' or 'grand', believing it's not safe for us to feel better than average, it's certainly risky to say it out loud. By admitting (even to ourselves) that we are happy, we put ourselves in the firing line, opening to vulnerability and so much more. If they see it, they may take it. As a result, finding happiness can feel dangerous, so downplaying success, joy, love ... whatever ... may be a logical thing to do in a bid to protect it. If no one sees it, you can keep it.

The idea that people are more afraid of success than failure always seemed a little trite to me, but I believe it now. I believe that we are contained by fear and that we restrict ourselves to live in whatever shitty little box someone decided we should stay in. If we don't budge we are deemed 'good', 'well behaved' – we are accepted. If we don't question who put us in the box or why we continue to hang out there, then we can't break out because we don't even see the walls. Yes, you feel a bit claustrophobic – slightly smothered even – and there's a nagging feeling that this isn't quite right but you can't put your finger on it and you're knackered anyway so it's easier to just stay in the unidentified box and buy clothes you don't need for parties you don't want to go to, so that the little hole inside you will stop feeling so gape-y!

According to Marianne Williamson in *A Return to Love*, it's not actually that difficult to feel positive feelings or think positive thoughts. It's our default state apparently; at least it's how we arrived ... just listen to a tone-deaf kid singing daft songs at 6am. The problem is that we resist them – these good and simple feelings make us feel naive or guilty – so we talk ourselves out of them or maybe we feel ourselves out of them! As Marianne notes, 'to the ego, there is no greater crime than claiming our natural inheritance.' The ego tells us, if I'm rich, someone else must be poor. If I become successful, someone's feelings might get hurt. If I experience big love, it may highlight someone else's loneliness. Who am I to have it all anyway? Maybe it will be threatening, and people won't like me any more. These are just some of the arguments the ego leaks and without interception these thoughts become beliefs that drive our behaviours on a subconscious level and determine our perception of the world and our experience living in it. In response, we usually shrink.

Historically it may have been very risky to get 'above your station'; it could quite literally threaten your survival if you get chucked out of the nest or the cave, but this threat is not real any more. You are safe. It's OK to have good things. You are worthy of good things. You are deserving. You can have a big and beautiful life. You can live the way you want. It's OK to thrive. You are safe.

Good Things

Give yourself good things. Why is it that you so readily chat shit to yourself, about yourself? You run on empty. You expect so much and give little in return. When did you decide you are undeserving? Who decided that? Why does the very act of nourishing yourself, of caring for yourself, seem indulgent rather than standard. Sissy. Dramatic. Needy. Demanding. When did you figure out that you are not worthy of basic comfort? Of basic care? And when will you change?

You know it's only you who can, right? You can read all the quotes and every last book, you can have all the conversations but only you can make a choice about how you treat you. How you treat yourself. Not just a takeaway, a new moisturiser or a pair of shoes for a job well done – when will you make a choice to hold yourself every day. Without expectation or condition. Just to love yourself for being. To love yourself when you have spots! To take your face kindly in your hands and accept your imperfections, your glorious humanness.

Can you look at yourself naked? At that body that carries you every single day. The one you starve and stuff depending on your mood. Undereating or overindulging. Pushing, pulling, squeezing. When will you see this body as your home and not a vessel? When will you recognise that the touch you crave is something you can give yourself? You can hold yourself in a loving embrace, you can gently guide and comfort your body like you might another human. You can look upon your flesh with soft eyes and wonder, without harsh judgements.

When will you allow yourself to be seen without a filter? To know that your worth doesn't lie in likes. To understand deeply that you are seen and held and watched even when you don't have your face on. Will it take much longer for you to accept that you will not disappear if you do not appear online. You are not for consumption. You are not a bowl of chips to be salivated over, compared with other chips consumed weeks, months, years ago . . . never. You are whole. Babe, you're a potato, with those eyes and sprouts and imperfections. You are endless possibility. You are whatever you want to be. You are limitless and loveable and fucking amazing . . . especially with butter.

Who Run The World

I am grateful for my women all over the world. For the ones who hold me silently in their minds, the ones who hold me while I cry, who call me back when I lash out, who love me even when I act out. For my sisters whose blood runs through me, the ones who built me. The old glorious ones who are part of my messy patchwork quilt. The ones who drank boxes of wine in the back of vans with me, who told me I looked cute when I absolutely did NOT. The ones who lent me their straighteners and Heather Shimmer. The ones who let me in. Who kicked me out. The ones who spoke to my soul only for a brief time but who stuck around in me forever. The ones who recognised me in an instant, from another life or another time. Love at first sight.

I am moved by this moment because I didn't always have this. Except that I did. I always, always had the best of friends. I just didn't know it, didn't allow myself to feel it, to receive them. That's the mad thing with this life and these minds of ours: when they chat unchecked, they tell you stories that are often built on untruths. It's funny that we long for and crave things that we have right now if only we could stop to feel them. The fullness of them. The potential for them to heal us and nurture us. The love you need is everywhere you turn. It is all of you; you just need to open.

So Deliciously Needy

Self-care is born out of self-knowledge. Knowing and honouring your needs and how they change daily, hourly. Honouring your humanness. Giving yourself what you need. Not just knowing your wonder but also knowing your limits. Aiming for a life without limits doesn't mean you don't have any. Recognise them and give yourself space and compassion to exist.

It is not enough to read the books and watch the docs and know the stuff. Of course you need to understand intellectually but the growth happens when it becomes part of you – when what the mind understands becomes part of how you move in the world. Compassion is an inside job; it is not just how you behave towards yourself and others but how you think and feel about yourself and others. Our minds and bodies are not separate. So how you treat yourself, how you think about yourself spills into every other area of your life. Mind yourself, manage your expectations, build yourself up and give yourself permission to pause.

I once, in anticipation of a very busy year, decided to do double therapy sessions (two a week). I understand what an immense privilege this is even if it sometimes feels like torture! Like a bootcamp for my head, I would cross the line at Christmas – stealthy and sure-footed, solid. I would be 'done', I would be 'fixed' (that old chestnut!). My therapist observed that, in my mind, being 'fixed' was being finished, sorted, without need, and gently suggested that maybe being 'fixed' was recognising what I needed and giving myself that. It was an oddly profound moment. This was something I genuinely had never even considered before. It felt wild. Novel. And a bit dangerous.

It was also infuriating as it signalled the end of my modus operandi – my misheld belief that I could do it all, that I was without limits. But mostly I felt relief, finally being given permission (even if it was against my will) to *need*. Not just in a moment of weakness or a period of flux, not just in a crisis when a deliciously dramatic family intervention may be called for, but all the time. To discover that, as a human, needs are constant. They are ever-changing but they are ever. Always. That is the constant. That realisation made me relax, like I could stop holding my breath, recognising maybe for the first time ever that needs are there to be satisfied not squashed. If someone in a meeting is shouting to be heard and people ignore them, the shouting doesn't stop even if it goes inwards; it turns into an angry hum and builds resentment. If, however, their point is heard, they can sit back down and relax; the shouting is no longer necessary. Need is the same. Once your needs are met, they do not grow ever more demanding, raging incessantly and swallowing you whole. They sit quietly only to nudge you when you forget. They guide you back to yourself if you will only listen.

Some examples of Universal Human Needs,
just in case, like me, you forget!

Physical
air, food, sleep, movement, shelter, sex, water, touch

Connection
acceptance, affection, belonging, closeness,
intimacy, love, support, respect, mutuality

Play
adventure, joy, humour, spontaneity, opportunity

Harmony
balance, ease, peace, equality

Honesty

authenticity, clarity, integrity, trust, openness

Meaning

awareness, hope, learning, purpose, self-expression,
creativity, mourning, celebration

Giving yourself all of these on any given day can just feel like another impossible task that's never getting done but being aware of them is half the battle. Aiming to recognise that many basic human needs are considered luxuries, creating space and giving yourself what you need as often as possible, is what we're going for. Start to look at the things that are really important to you – what makes you feel nourished and charged and able to hold all of the madness of a week. What are you missing when your edges feel frayed. It's so easy to say 'I'm knackered, I'll be grand after a good kip' and there's a lot to be said for that but let's try to dig a bit deeper (daily) and give ourselves what we need in order to thrive. Fill your cup up so you can spill it all over the shop – when *you* choose!

Sad Sandwich

The idea of finding time for infra-red saunas and cosy nights of nurturing may give you more anxiety than they would fix but it's the simplest things that allow us to move at our best through the world. Self-care is bandied around as a cure-all for anyone feeling overwhelmed with life but I'm more into self-compassion. Obviously I am still buying a sauna in what looks like a body bag because it promises to make me look younger and sleep better but ... I'm also trying to give myself the most basic things, the things that I often overlook until I'm on the floor.

I film on location a lot. That means I'm up and down the country, often having dinner in a hotel room or grabbing lunch at a petrol station. I have this weird thing with sandwiches for as long as I can remember. Seriously, I hate sandwiches. I have always hated them. The stodgy breadiness of them, the soggy fillings, the dry crusts! When I was in primary school, I would swap my wholesome 'boring' sandwiches with Emma Fagan, who would buy me Monster Munch and a Stinger bar in Tara News. No one knew; everyone was happy. But this weird disdain for sandwiches didn't seem to disappear, and, guess what, I think it was about more than ambivalence towards the trusty slice pan. Sandwiches were a symbol of need, a reminder that I was not an island; my chucking of them some small act of defiance and rebellion. A statement to myself and my little mind that I was self-sufficient and didn't need these mother-made bread slabs when I could cleverly swap them for some no-strings-attached penny sweets. As long as I didn't accept the sandwiches, I could convince myself I didn't need any-thing or anyone. And that puffed me up in a way that bread couldn't.

My friend Jimbo is a treasure; he started off as a run-ner on our show and I'm pretty sure he'll soon be my boss (and yours too, probably). When we're filming, he's the one who brings coffee before you start to wilt, who calls to ask which Rennie you need ('is it for heartburn or gas?'), he makes sure everyone has what they need and he does it with a smile. He is unwavering in his commitment to making sure everyone's looked after. I used to worry about Jimbo. Has he eaten himself or forgotten with all his fussing over everyone else? Is he working too hard? Is he safe to drive if he's tired?

During the pandemic, we all had a few months at home (obviously) and, when we reunited, I noticed Jimbo had lost weight. A lot of weight, which was weird because in my mind he didn't have any to lose. He looked skinny. A strapping 6ft-something but his cheekbones were razor-sharp now. I wanted to feed him biscuits. He chose a sandwich he had made earlier. To me, a packed lunch had always felt utterly depressing – life's just too short to endure a soggy salad or a pre-dressed baguette and some smashed crisps. I would rather order in or nip out, or go without.

It turned out Jimbo had stomach issues and had to cut out a lot of food in order to sort himself out – sugar, dairy, grains and gluten. The works. Every day we shot, he would organise our lunch – order in noodles or grab salad bowls on the run; every day Jimbo would wait until everyone was satisfied and then eat his 'sad sandwich' alone. I felt sorry for him. The visual of him carefully unwrapping his lunch brought me back to the sad sandwiches rejected at the bottom of my schoolbag or exchanged for sugar. Those sandwiches were made with intention and love by my mam while I slept. She was thinking of me before I went to school and sending me off with a nourishing little cling-film-wrapped feast. She was giving me something I needed even if I didn't recognise it or couldn't accept it at the time. I just thought I didn't like sandwiches but this was what Oprah would call an 'aha!' moment.

The next time Jimbo whipped out his 'sad sandwich' (by the way, this was his term not mine) and winced, I told him I loved that he brought a packed lunch every day. It was a true and majestic act of self-love, not for Instagram, not for anyone but him. The act of caring enough about himself to plan a day in advance. To have the right bread in the house and enough to fill it, to think about doing it and have a box to take it in. It might not be perfect or beautifully presented, it might not even taste that good, but he cared enough about himself to make it, and that felt like everything: to honour himself with what his body needs ... nourishment and consideration and kindness. Self-love is not a petal bath or a monthly massage, it's not bottomless brunch or a new handbag (although all of these things may nourish you in ways, they are not a substitute for everyday kindness aimed at yourself); Jimbo's 'sad sandwich' is what radical self-love is all about.

These thoughtful daily acts are something many of us take for granted; I know I certainly do. Perhaps their significance gets overlooked in their simplicity. The pandemic brought into sharp focus the value of everyday moments and the value of their cumulative effect. The big gestures, the expensive quick-fixes, the shiny treatments, all seem a little hollow or maybe we just realise that to rely on those sporadic gems while neglecting the day-to-day isn't really sustainable. We realised, pretty much at the same time, that days punctuated by a 'nice lunch' or a walk in the park can actually feed your soul and heal you just a bit. The collective pause allowed us to consider our needs, to actually ask our-selves 'what do I need today?', what would make me happy or satisfied or at least keep me sane? How do I nourish myself in a way that's not flashy but wholesome and true. Can I love myself enough to honour my needs every day? Can I give myself a humble sandwich?

What is your version of the 'sad sandwich' and when are you going to start feeding yourself?

- Write a list of the little things daily that fill you up. Is it getting up a bit earlier to have a shower in peace? Is it finding time to have dinner with your girlfriends once a month? Is it a phone call without distractions or a doc-tor's appointment you keep putting off because you don't want to seem dramatic.

- Start to recognise your needs and at least try to fulfil them, no matter how insignificant they seem. Added up, unmet needs result in a sense of overwhelm so check in regularly.

- Don't be afraid (or ashamed) to ask for help.

Rest Glorious Rest

If your batteries aren't charged, it doesn't matter how fabulous your life is; it will be impossible to enjoy it, to experience every juicy moment. Being there is not enough; you want to be *in* it, squeezing every last drop out of life, but it won't happen if you're drunk on exhaustion. It's not cute or heroic to exist on minimal sleep, I'm not sure when that happened? FUN FACT: you'll die quicker from lack of sleep than from lack of food. So stop dicking around on Netflix and go to bed.

The most beautiful gift you can give yourself is the gift of rest. In a world obsessed with production and progressing and pushing, it is an act of glorious self-love to lie down and listen to your heart. Last Sunday I had a nap; I know, wild! Except that it kind of was. I generally talk a good game; I have created rituals and routines that ensure I make time for myself but it doesn't come naturally and I have to fight against the idea that I must constantly be moving, doing, sorting, making, producing. That rest, in and of itself, is pointless and lazy.

I'm not sure how we got to the point where it feels anarchic to just down tools and take a break. Our nervous

"Start to take courageous, imperfect action daily to train your nervous system to take more and more action in the present moment"

Mastin Kipp

systems have been running on overdrive, running on empty for years, maybe even decades, and we have reached our collective limits. Obviously this has been exacerbated by the pandemic but, in another way, we have experienced a slowing down that many of us will miss and fight to hold onto.

Remember when you would wake at 6am, check your emails en route to the gym, do a gruelling spin class (further spiking the adrenals), rush to work pumped on coffee, 'go, go, go' all day long, 'yes, yes, yes', nothing is too much? We react all day to others' demands. Then we leave work frazzled so we can rush to eat a meal with a friend who's equally burnt out or leg it to do bedtime while frantically trying to sort the house and make dinner and not be an asshole. Tick. Tick. Tick. We lie down and sleep fitfully, our exhausted bodies begging to be heard, but when you have spent forever ignoring those twinges, those whispers from inside, eventually they stop. You lose connection with your basic needs. You live in survival mode, feeding the beast rather than yourself.

But if you shut your mind up for a little while and tune in to your body, it will tell you everything you need to know. If you manage to sit with yourself and really listen you always know what you need and you also know when you've neglected yourself, and when you must stop.

I have a friend who is wildly in tune with herself –
four kids, and a husband who works away all the time, and
she always seems so together and so sane and so damn
relaxed. Obviously I want to buy whatever she's selling but
she's not a faddist; she doesn't read GOOP or eat crystals
for breakfast – she's the opposite. She listens only to her 87-
year-old dad's sage advice: 'When you're tired, go to sleep.
When you're sick, lie down. When you're sad, cry.' Seems so
simple and yet so few of us allow ourselves the luxury of
listening to what we need in any given moment, and giving
ourselves just that. Allowing ourselves to wilt under the
weight of expectation and the relentless pace that has
become so familiar.

We don't honour our bodies or our cycles; instead
we treat ourselves like battery hens built to produce every
hour on the hour (and the yolk better be bright yellow). At
no other time in history have we been expected to work for
10-/12-hour days, ALWAYS ON, forever delivering, forever
reactive. Yes, there were periods of great work (we harvested
in summer) but in winter we hunkered down; we recuper-
ated. People were allowed to exhale. When was the last time
you fully EXHALED?

Check in with yourself a couple of times a day, once
if this seems radical to begin with. Pause and allow yourself
to listen to what you need. Drop your expectations, tear up

your to-do list and sit down. Let it all go to shit around you, let the laundry pile up today – see it, accept it and let it go. Take 15 minutes (or 5), don't scroll, don't read. LIE DOWN. Wherever you can. In fact, lie down WHENEVER you can, open your arms and surrender to it all. You are not a machine; you are a divine human. A human being.

Stop doing. Start being.

The Science Bit . . .

When reading, listening to podcasts and scrolling holistic therapy accounts on Instagram, I kept hearing references to the nervous system – growing the nervous system to be able to 'call in more', self-regulating, homeostasis. It was like another language to me and I didn't really get it. I was trying to heal my head, feed my mind, create from my thoughts, but this seemed to be all about the body. I would have ignored it if I could but it seemed to appear everywhere I turned.

And of course it should be obvious that there would be a connection between experiences *experienced* in the body as well as held in the mind. They are one and the same. We are both body and mind. We can try to separate them and isolate them with different treatments, exercises and modalities but they feed each other and healing one while denying the other leaves you only half-baked, a little torn, not altogether whole.

So, the nervous system? The nervous system controls everything you do, including breathing, walking, thinking and feeling. This system is made up of your brain, spinal cord and all the nerves of your body. These nerves carry the messages to and from the body, so the brain can interpret them and take action. The autonomic nervous system acts independently of the body's consciousness. There are two main divisions – the sympathetic and the parasympathetic – which are opposing but connected. Still with me???

The SYMPATHETIC is associated with arousal, stress, heightened anxiety, high alert, foot on the pedal – this is fight/flight/freeze mode. The PARASYMPATHETIC, in contrast, helps to keep us calm, it signals safety, it offers relaxation, healing, relief – this is rest/digest mode. How quickly you go from a heightened state of stress back to homeostasis (your body's optimum state) is determined by your body's acquired capacity to downregulate the nervous system. I think of it as talking yourself off the ledge, breathing yourself off the ledge. Calmly, gently and confidently knowing that you are not in danger and you can cope. You are OK and guiding yourself back to level ground. But most of us are so detached from our bodies that we don't even realise we're permanently living in this heightened state, doing untold damage in the pursuit of just doing.

Our ability to take ourselves back to base is known as self-regulating and our proficiency at doing that is dependent on many things. But it's something we must learn, it's not innate. Trauma prevents the nervous system from regulating itself, bringing the body back to a place of calm and safety after stress.

Traumatic events come in many forms and affect people at different levels. It could be a flippant comment never addressed, sibling rivalry or playground bullying. We often assume trauma is about the very worst human experiences but as children our dependence on others means that small rejections and everyday upsets can feel like life or death. The little things are everything.

Babies are born with the ability to hit stress (crying, fussing etc) but they do not have, inbuilt, the capacity to self-soothe at birth. The baby's nervous system develops the ability to calm down through thousands and thousands of supportive, soothing interactions with caregivers. At first, the caregiver is essentially functioning as the child's parasympathetic nervous system – rubbing and rocking and loving them back to comfort. The development of this 'braking system' continues throughout childhood, through continued positive interactions that meet the child's needs ... but very often those needs are not met, for whatever reason, leaving many of us adults with the inability to come back to centre effectively.

There are a whole host of reasons why you may not have learned/been taught how to self-soothe or downregulate. Post-traumatic stress, postpartum depression in the mum, bullying that went unnoticed, a chaotic household, parents who were addicts, wartime, a family bereavement, poverty. The result is the system getting stuck in the 'on' position (fight or flight), overstimulated and unable to calm. Stress hormones, cortisol and adrenaline, are released. Anxiety, anger, restlessness, panic, and hyperactivity can all result when you stay in this ready-to-react mode for too long. It's exhausting, so many of us choose to escape these feelings of stress and anxiety through booze, drugs, eating disorders etc. But distracting yourself from the discomfort of 'fight or flight' is not the same as entering 'rest and digest.'

But the good news is that you can learn to comfort yourself, how to soothe yourself. Great things happen when you come back to base. Our breath is full, slow, and deep. The digestive system works well. The body can focus on repair, including reduction of inflammation, tissue repair, and hormone production. You will feel present and alive and warm and fuzzy and safe.

Practical tips to help heal the nervous system

- **Lookout**

  Check yourself. When you sit to relax in meditation or just to chill out – actually wherever you are – look around, check behind you, take in your surrounds. Perceiving your whole environment sends a message that you are safe. You've checked your surroundings for danger. You can breathe.

- **Havening**

  Basically go hug yourself, babe. Place both hands on opposite shoulders, crossing your arms in front of you. Apply gentle pressure to your shoulders, then move them down your biceps slowly until you come to your elbow, then repeat! (This is also using bilateral stimulation.) There are nerve endings right under the surface of your skin cells on the upper body. When you apply pressure there, it creates delta waves in the brain (the same brain waves produced during deep REM sleep) and it slows the beta wave pattern down. Hug everyone you can, especially yourself.

- **Deep Breathing**

  When you sleep, you breathe into your lower belly and beyond, stimulating the vagus nerve and telling your body that you are safe. Bad posture, a desk job that has you bent over for much of the day, can cut off oxygen supply to the vagus nerve, which would stimulate positive feel-good hormones. Throughout the day, make sure you get up and breathe deeply through the belly and the booty, triggering that vagus nerve and rinsing your body clean of cortisol and other stress hormones.

- **Unclench Your Jaw**

  It's usually tight when we're poised to fight and often we don't even realise we're clenching. Check in and slacken your lovely jaws as soon as you feel the burn, ideally before that!

- **EFT – Emotional Freedom Technique**

  Tapping on acupressure points in the body to stimulate those positive brainwave frequencies (delta waves) and releasing the positive chemicals into the brain (serotonin and dopamine). Start at the top of your head and tap gently. Move to the temple, then between the eyebrows, forehead, cheekbone, then above the lip, then the chin, then the chest, then right under the armpit, top of the wrist and finally, right above the wrist on your pinky finger side (the karate chop point!). Particularly good for heightened states and panic attacks, and you can do it in the loo.

- **Singing**

  This is a powerful way to uplift your nervous system when you feel low. Find your favourite song, put it on and sing like a beast! Crank it up in the shower and set yourself up for the day. Oh, and while you're in there, stick it on freezing for a minute before you finish.

The Anti-Hustle

'If you stop producing, you will not disappear.' You can lie down and breathe deep, rest and refill your cup. It's not lazy, it's vital.

No man is an island. No woman is an island. But for a long time I was one! In the middle of the Irish Sea, choppy as fuck all around and pretty isolated. Most of the time I wanted to escape to an actual island to lie down in a dark room or underneath an umbrella in the morning sun.

I remember reading an article by some woman talking about holidays and how we now think of holidays as a break from real life. We fill our diaries with two weeks' worth of work before we go and work overtime on return to make up for our absence. I spent my honeymoon sneaking to the toilet to check my phone. We had a week because I had to get back to work. Our precious honeymoon was stolen, almost an inconvenience, and I felt angry and resentful but also guilty as hell. We'd just got married, for fuck's sake. This is IT! If we can't properly switch off and enjoy newly-wedded bliss, what's the point? But the point was that I couldn't plug myself out for long enough to feel anything of real value. As long as I kept running and striving, as long as I was producing I would be OK. The honeymoon was a faraway destination; I was sure when I reached it I would be full as a bus and happy as a clam. I was, on paper, but I was so out of the habit of being with myself, being with my husband, I didn't really know how to 'be'.

Holidays for so many of us are an escape and a period of recovery rather than an adventure. A holiday is no longer a time to feed the soul, deepen relationships through shared experience, open the mind; it's just an expensive lie-in, a recovery from the relentless pace that has become our 'normal'.

Recently we spent two long days travelling to get from London to Cork. Through Wales, onto the boat, disembark in Dublin, onward to Cork. I didn't sleep once while we were moving! A two-year-old in the back helped me stay alert but I realised that what now felt quite easy (i.e. staying awake) was impossible just a few years ago. It was a running joke that as soon as I got into a moving vehicle I slept, like I was under some sort of spell.

Myself and my husband got engaged in India. There, we spent days travelling in the wildest conditions; along mountain edges, up against trucks with elephants on the back, overtaking on cliff tops, enough to make me sick just thinking about it but the truth is I don't remember any of it because while he clung to the back seat, praying we'd some-how manage to make it out alive, I slept. I was constantly exhausted. My 'downtime' was writing a column or pitching an idea to someone about something. It was drumming up work. In my mind, if I wasn't on show it wasn't really work, but I was completely whacked. And I expected that level of madness from everyone around me. The same commitment, the same sacrifice. Needs, especially personal ones, were not welcome in my world.

I once sacked an assistant because she said she wouldn't work on Sunday. I rolled my eyes and wished her well, positive she would fail since she wasn't prepared to give her all. In reality I was raging with jealousy that some-one younger, less experienced, less 'successful' dared to protect her own downtime, dared to value her actual life over her working life. I was affronted and insulted; actually, I was disgusted. It took me many years to apply some level of boundary to my own working week. To put on an Out of Office and respect it.

Rest was a foreign word. It was something I didn't have time for. My self-imposed deadline was relentlessly driving me on. Barely on the right side of 30 and already too late to the game. I was against the clock, a feeling I always had, like a timebomb, like I was running from a tsunami.

I put this pressure on myself but it's everywhere if you want to feel it. I briefly shaved a year off my 'public' age because at 30 I was deemed too old to do 'cool' things (by myself!) We fetishise youth. We idolise 17-year-old billionaires and child prodigies. '30 under 30' lists celebrate mighty success but for people who haven't even discovered what they want from life or how to show up, these lists are salt in the collective wound. Of course, we are all somewhat in awe of the 'unicorns', the overnight successes. We tell ourselves that their success was good luck or God-given. We tell ourselves that if we haven't got it sorted, the luck has run out, or that God skipped us in the queue. What if we chilled the fuck out and thought about life as a trip around the world rather than a skip across the road. Where are the 70 over 70 lists? Faster and younger doesn't mean better; there can be hard falls with quick rises. The people we should celebrate are the ones who have picked themselves up over and over and over again. Who have had to dig deep and withstand the pain of failure and defeat and rejection – the ones who are courageous enough to keep coming back for more.

You don't need to constantly push and pitch and hustle and drive. I always thought that as soon as I stopped working I would just become invisible, uninteresting, unloveable! What a load of balls. You have SO much to offer that has absolutely nothing to do with what you do for work. Don't look around and believe that those who are relentlessly busy are somehow more valuable or happier. Busyness is a very socially acceptable way to run away from yourself. It's much harder to actually just hang out with yourself.

Enough

A few years ago I was a guest on a chat show in Ireland. It's hosted by Tommy Tiernan, a comedian and broadcaster who I adore. The premise of the show is that he doesn't know what guests are coming on, there's no script, no prep, no publicist-approved questions, just the two of you. Maybe he knows you, or knows who you are; maybe he doesn't. And with me, he didn't have a clue. Which was a little sucker punch to my ego! He wondered if I was a writer (I am not Patricia Scanlan FYI). We talked, had a laugh, some of it was random, some of it was uncomfortable, some of it was aimless. As an interviewer it can be excruciating to be interviewed.

I could tell he was running out of places to go or was that me? I had left my daughter in London, the first time we were separated by an ocean. I missed her deeply but I was so out of touch with myself that I didn't know why I felt so sensitive, so sad, so fragile.

My head said: 'get a grip. You chose this.' That was a line I heard a lot; I still hear it. 'You chose this, stop complaining.' Like there was no world where I could feel two things at the same time. Happy to be there while also sad to not be at home. Thankful for a job I love as well as guilty for having to leave. I couldn't acknowledge the loss of a thing. The choosing of one thing over another. The choice. My choice and the responsibility that came with it. The consequences. So instead of giving them space, and recognising what I needed, I swallowed them and they leaked out in ways I couldn't control or understand.

'Where does the ambition come from?' Tommy asked, like a punch in the gut.

I laughed.

'Maybe I wouldn't ask a man that,' he followed up.

He wouldn't, to be fair. But I sat in that chair in front of an audience with this deeply intuitive, gifted man looking into my soul and exposing me in front of the nation.

'The relentless drive . . . where does that come from?' he asked again.

I wanted to tell him to fuck off and mind his own business. I think I said, 'Unresolved childhood trauma,' and laughed again, but it felt so hideously personal – a judgement on my life and my choices.

'Are you happy?' he asked.

Sweet Jesus, when will this stop? What kind of a question is that anyway? Am I happy; what does that even mean? NO, I'M MISERABLE. I am a shit mother who's abandoned her baby at home to come to do a job for money, not love. My husband has been picking up the slack. I've been hiding in the bath, hiding from my life. Hiding from the failure I believe I've brought on myself. I don't know who I am. I don't know why I'm here and I am so deeply, deeply upset that I don't consider myself enough to ask if this is too much right now. That I care so little about my own mental health that instead of an early night and a Facetime with my little family I have tried to fill every minute with something; that 'I actually chose this'!

I chose to sit on a chair under a glaring spotlight at one of the most vulnerable moments in my life. I knew I shouldn't have; I wasn't ready. But I overruled that weak little voice that wished to hold me and threw myself onto that stage. For a brief second I thought I would cry, right there on the velvet chair. And if I started I might never stop.

Sometimes we can do 'hard things', as Glennon Doyle calls them. We can take the pressure, we can bear the load, we can grow through the trial. Get out there and dance and sing and dazzle them with a smile. We can go to bed happy that we pulled it out of the bag. But sometimes we can allow ourselves the kindness we would offer a friend.

We can allow ourselves to admit that it's just too much. That we are not machines who light up on demand. We can break down in a safe, warm place. In a velvet chair ... just without the spotlight.

Chapter Four

How Fear and Comparison Rob Our Joy

Doubting Debbie

Today, I'm sitting at my desk, a new desk, a desk I bought for writing. A gift in advance of the act. Up until now scrawled notes on pieces of paper or words autocorrected on the notes in my phone. Little nuggets of inspiration that feel powerful late at night but in the morning make me cringe. They are nothing.

Like the boldness I'm possessed by when I'm drunk, looking in the mirror and saying 'wow, you look FAB' only to see the pictures the following day of a sweaty, shiny mess. How can things that feel so solid, so full of optimism, suddenly look like crap? I contemplate writing drunk. It's worked for some people but it seems wildly out of step with my intention. Not that I care if you're drunk; do what you do. I just know that what I'm seeking is to feel 'GREAT' in the cold light of day, without a filter or a ring light or a puddle of tequila in my gut. I actually want my gut to believe on the deepest level that what I have to say is of value, regardless of the light. That actually the shine, the sweat, the imperfection is what is most 'me'.

I type. Then delete. And start again. I bite my nails. Actually the skin around my nails, a filthy habit that's given me a slightly crooked tooth such is the ferocity with which I commit. Sometimes I am so out of step with what I feel that a bloody finger is the first thing that alerts me to the fact that I'm not OK, or at least not as OK as I like to be. It is a little sign. A nod to remind me to go inside.

There are others too.

- Procrastination
- Eating without tasting
- Scrolling without stopping
- Spending without thinking
- Looking without seeing
- Needing a bath NOW
- Screening calls
- Working relentlessly
- Disconnecting

These just sound like things I do on any given day and I thought they were until I realised they weren't. Until I realised that these things were distractions to take me away from the feeling in the pit of my stomach. From the feeling of fear that I am not enough. From the anticipation of too much work or not enough. From the missing of something or someone. From pain as yet unidentified. Discomfort too uncomfortable to confront. 'Business' has been my default state for as long as I can remember. Writing lists and looking forward. Looking forward to work until I had to do it. Looking forward to dinner until I had to eat it. Looking forward to a holiday until I got there. Overthinking, overcommitting, over-expecting, over easy eggs scrambled in my head.

The body does not have the capacity to overthink, only the mind does, so when the mind is foggy or flighty, when it's racing ahead and pulling you into panic or unease – raining all over your little parade – you can stop it. I have learned to shift my presence to my physical body. To take a big, fat, delicious deep breath and remember I am here NOW. To properly ground myself. I have nowhere else to be, nothing else to do, no one else to look at. Look in.

Faking It

'Fake it till you make it' was a mantra I lived by for a very long time. It was the tattoo I'd have gotten; the slogan I touted with pride. It felt triumphant and bolshy – the thing that doers do. Fake it till you make it. Fake it. Fake what? Fake your skill? Fake your experience? Fake your opinion? It's hard to fully understand what exactly I was faking but I definitely was.

We hear a lot about impostor syndrome – how everyone feels it to varying degrees. It may feel unique to you but ask your friends, ask your family, ask your boss . . . we're all clueless! It seems to be part of the gig called life and not just a personal affliction, so take a deep breath.

Statistically, men are more clueless than women but they're also less self-aware (this is science; I won't hear it questioned). Study after study has shown that men routinely overestimate their ability to do a job while women are overwhelmingly conservative when it comes to selling themselves and their skills. Maybe growing up in a house full of females meant I was less aware of the roles we were supposed to play – modesty trumping all for the ladies; healthy aggression and over-inflation of the self obligatory

"To the inferior eye everyone else is greater. Others are more beautiful, brilliant and gifted than you. The inferior eye is always looking away from its own treasures. It can never celebrate its own presence and potential. The inferior eye is blind to its secret beauty. The human eye was never designed to look up in a way that inflates the other to superiority, nor to look down reducing the other to inferiority. To look someone in the eye is a nice testament to truth, courage and expectation. Each one stands on common but different ground"

John O'Donoghue, *Anam Cara*

for the lads. I think it freed me a bit but impostor syndrome still hangs around a lot.

Have you ever felt like you don't belong somewhere or you haven't earned your place at the table? Like you're about to be found out. Well, that lingering feeling that a boss or colleague or friend is going to knock on your door or slide into your DMs with a gentle 'we're done' is a sure-fire way of sapping any joy in life. Believing your potential is key to doing brilliant and scary things that make you grow and level-up but it's also important to be tuned in to your limitations.

Over the years I may have been a little flamboyant with the truth; perhaps on occasion I embellished and painted a slightly 'fuller' picture around what I had done on my CV! I would 'chance' it, surely the only way to get experience was to get experience? I didn't know I could do it but I *knew* I could do it. It was based on a feeling rather than any concrete proof. There were things I was just sure about, so I allowed myself to up-sell, to leave small untruths unchecked, and allowed people to believe things that helped me progress. I backed myself and it was my filthy little secret. I basically leaned into my masculine. I pretended I knew how to do the thing before I actually knew; I believed it was the feminist thing to do. To lead with the false confidence that most men exhibit in professional interview situations. A small triumph in a big, cold world.

But the thing about building foundations on a field of fairy dust is that when you get shaken the dust disappears. It was never really there. And what you're left with is a structure that may have glistened but was hollow all along. Don't get me wrong, I am a firm believer in doing the things, ALL of them (well, most of them) before you feel 'ready.' It is, in my opinion, the only way to *get* ready. Readiness isn't a gift bestowed upon us; it's something we earn in the doing. But there is a difference between striding out of your comfort zone with at least an eye on some shore and launching yourself headlong off a cliff with no promise of a parachute.

The discomfort I craved so much was oddly sadistic. If it felt hideously intimidating, I wanted to do it. If I was shaking with terror it was proof I *had* to do it. Like I could have nothing 'good' without enduring the terror or pain of feeling overwhelmed. Ease was never something I valued or craved. I equated success with surviving harsh or at the very least challenging conditions. I also held the belief that this kind of discomfort that I so regularly sought out could only be eradicated by facing the fear head on, and the dogged commitment to facing it, I felt, gave me an edge.

Not the One

A good example of this is when I started working on *The One Show* after a meeting with the boss where I came armed with a notebook and a tonne of ideas, none of which ever made it to air. But he liked my enthusiasm. I was fearless and energetic and full of optimism. I had been trying to get a meeting with the producers for years; I had reached out and pitched to anyone who would listen as I was sure I should be on that show. Live TV was where I came alive; it felt utterly natural to me and I loved it. I was also good at it. I was meant to be doing it. I knew on some deep level that this was the case so when they asked if I had presented a live studio show before, I responded without a flinch: 'Sure I've done it, in Ireland, loads of it, love it!' I lied. Next question . . .

And so I got a gig as their roving reporter. I spent a couple of months visiting damp fields and East London markets. I interviewed the farmer who once kicked Rihanna out of his field for dressing and dancing 'inappropriately', I learned how gold bars were made, and I almost burned a woman alive on a windy peak in Somerset while lighting a 'beacon' for the Queen's birthday. (Thankfully we both survived.)

A few months later, out of the blue, I got a call saying the BBC wanted me to present the main show. The live show. Their flagship show that is watched by millions every evening. I would be sitting with people as they had their dinner, got their kids ready for bed, settled in for the night. I had absolutely no idea what I was doing so obviously I said 'YES', immediately.

Within days I found myself sitting on that famous green sofa hosting one of the biggest shows on British telly. I had talked my way into it, which would be fine except that I was flying blind. Because I had told the team that I had the necessary experience, there was no hand holding mine. The assumption (rightly so, based on our discussion) was that I was a professional so they should just let me do my thing. The only problem was I didn't know what my thing was or how the hell to do it. I had neglected once again to have a quiet word with myself, to ask 'what do you need here?' Instead, I turned away from myself and towards the camera.

I sat on that couch with studio lights glaring, an autocue on, a bunch of people in my ear, feeling totally out of my depth, but I dismissed those feelings because that's what I believed you had to do. Back yourself when you can.

Take an opportunity when it's presented. Face your fear. Take a leap etc. So I gritted my teeth. The light turned red, the trumpets sounded, I smiled and hoped for the best. And the 'best' became a reality. They loved me. I winged it in the way I always had. I was alive and the sheer recklessness of potentially fucking up my entire fledgling career live on TV was exhilarating. It was also one of the most stupid things I have ever done.

But … I got the gig. And I covered maternity leave on that very show. It was huge. A break and a half. A coup. An honour. A shambles … My foundations were rocky and it was too late to backtrack so I spent a long and lonely stint never once expressing fear or asking for the help or support I so desperately needed. I had built myself a little cage and wouldn't let anyone in. The team were amazing but I was riddled with anxiety. They would use technical terms in studio and I would have to google them on the sly (don't bother, you can't find the lingo). I was learning on the job but without a teacher.

I had tricked everyone into believing I was meant to be there – front and centre – but away from that studio I couldn't leave the house. I was a wreck. I was sitting in what I had told myself was the dream job, I was doing a gig that seemed impossible just a year before, I had won but I felt like shit.

For years I had convinced myself if I could beat the odds and get this job or that, if I could prove 'them' wrong and dazzle the disbelievers I would be happy. I would be SO, SO HAPPY. But I wasn't and the realisation that a job wouldn't fix me rocked me so hard, I was afraid I might not bounce back as I always had before.

It took me a few years to understand what it was that had impacted me so deeply. I assumed I had messed it up (I actually hadn't). I thought I had been given my shot and I'd blown it. I'd had the chance to 'live the dream' and I had turned it into a nightmare. The idea that I should arrive 'fully formed' was a lie that hovered around a lot. The notion that unless it was completely effortless and perfect then maybe it wasn't 'meant to be.' In this version there was no room for improvement or growth, no room for humanity. I either got it or I didn't. And if I didn't then on to the next.

It hit me a couple of years later when I was back on that same sofa with a peer and good friend who is an amazing broadcaster but hadn't done the show much. I observed her asking questions rather than secretly searching online. I heard her being offered guidance and encouragement, gentle criticism. She was aware of her limitations, open about them rather than ashamed and as a result she was able to give herself a break and allow for the mistakes and lessons that saw her improve. She also allowed herself some help. I had been so desperate to be seen as completely competent, unflappable, worthy of this shot that I was terrified to show anything but absolute confidence.

But the issue was I didn't feel deserving of any of it. I had created a situation that backed up a deep-rooted old belief that I'm not good enough. That I don't learn quick enough. That I'm lazy and entitled and sloppy. That I am stupid. The fear and nerves were proof that I wasn't good enough. The fluffed lines were proof that I didn't learn quickly enough. The reluctance to prepare properly in case I failed proved my arrogance. The mind is a trickster – don't believe everything you hear (in your head!). I was my own biggest troll except I couldn't mute or block myself, no matter how much I wanted to.

In truth, it was kind of thrilling to be dependent on others' opinions too. Like self-flagellation. I would open the comments and read through them, ignoring the good ones, and stamping the negative ones onto my mind. Like a rollercoaster, it was addictive, the lashings and slap-downs more exciting than any compliments. More memorable and more believable because the ideas I had about myself were pretty grim to begin with.

To look for the 'lesson' when you're in the eye of a shit-storm is a challenging thing to do and something I wasn't capable of for a long time. I still struggle. I saw other people accept difficult situations, embrace mistakes and so-called failures, fuelled by what they might learn, certain that there was some bigger thing at play, that it was part of a process. Or maybe they just had faith that they could survive. 'Everything happens for a reason!'. Instead, I chose to wallow in self-loathing and rub salt on that open wound (and I really got stuck in). It was like a psychic pile-on until finally I had enough.

I shifted out of self-pity and regret and began to see this whole experience as a gift. While I may not have been wholly grateful for it at the time, I could strive to look for the lesson. Sometimes we have to learn our lessons the hard way, and if we persistently ignore our souls' yearnings and override our basic needs, maybe the lessons need to be delivered in more dramatic fashion, a proper kick in the tits to wake you up.

Why horses wear blinkers

The tendency to look around and feel wanting is not unusual but it is miserable. Do you find you fixate on what others have, constantly comparing yourself and somehow always falling short? You know the way ... you've been out with your family or friends, had a lovely wholesome evening, you feel content and en route home pop onto Instagram, where you see 'everyone' having a bigger, brasher, infinitely better evening than you. It's not even a conscious thought but you're wondering why you weren't invited, why you don't seem to have friends who do fabulous all-nighters or ones with holiday homes you can use for free and have 'table-scaped' dinner parties on a Tuesday in April. It's because you're shit – or at least that's what the mind says and this is where gratitude can come in on a very practical level.

Social media is accused of a lot of things – reducing our productivity, creating zombies, making us tired, ruining our sleep, ruining our relationships, our ability to have meaningful conversation and killing human connection. That's quite a list and it's above my pay grade to comment on whether all or any of those beliefs are true but I do think that the ease with which we can compare ourselves to others – daily, hourly, constantly – has to have an impact on how we see ourselves.

'Comparison is the thief of joy,' as Theodore Roosevelt famously said. It stifles creativity and drive; it also stops you from doing what you know you can. It usually tries to stop you before you even start. And while that quote is clichéd as hell, printed on mugs and shared as motivation on Instagram (the irony!), it's also true.

Of course, we can't pin it all on social media. Comparison has been a human preoccupation since the dawn of time but previously it was the beautiful girl at school or the rich bloke in the village or the person in the tribe who was strongest, fittest, most appealing for procreation. It was basic, primal even, and there were limitations. Now, before we get out of bed, we can scroll through our phones and compare ourselves, our lives, our achievements (even our hypothetical plans) to those of the most accomplished individuals in the world: teenage global activists, billionaire social entrepreneurs, genetically blessed supermodels, or someone living in a forest with the perfect family and kids who aren't dicks. It's enough to make you give up before you even get up.

Wanting to keep up with the Joneses is not new. The term 'social comparison theory' was coined in 1954 by psychologist Leon Festinger, suggesting that people have an innate drive to evaluate themselves in comparison to others. People judge themselves relentlessly, often unconsciously and social comparison, or analysing the self in relation to others, is how we figure out where we are, where our attitudes and abilities lie on a scale. It's how we check if we're doing alright in this game of life!

We generally compare ourselves to people who appear somewhat like us in characteristics or capabilities. It's unusual to feel smug, for example, about being brighter than a five-year-old or better at football than your granny. The further away you feel from someone, the less likely you are to compare – or at least that's the theory.

So, when used constructively, comparison can motivate us and propel us forward, but relentless looking around and comparison can make you feel stuck and always in lack. Social comparison then needs to be used as fuel to empower rather than disable and you can help yourself with a little bit of thought and discipline and a good old-fashioned spring clean (but more than once a year).

Curating Your Crew

Instagram is somewhere that offers me endless inspiration. It's where I go to daydream about seaside houses with giant windows, elaborate feasts, overpriced shoes, overpriced art and exotic holidays. I save quotes and get insight into people's lives in a second that stays with me for days or weeks. But much like a wardrobe that gets jam-packed with things you once loved, you change, your perspective changes and people you once happily followed, jeans you once proudly wore, no longer fit you. We need to approach social media with the same intention to rid ourselves of things/accounts that make us feel bad about ourselves. Like doing a clear-out of your wardrobe, doing a ruthless clear-out of people you follow is essential. Curate, edit, cull – whatever you call it. That power is yours and if someone doesn't make you feel good then unfollow.

My rule is that I only follow people who help me feel empowered or emboldened, who allow me to expand my ideas around what is possible and then ones who offer pure escape (the animal and beautiful home accounts mostly).

You've probably heard of the idea that we become 'the average of the five people we spend the most time with', attributed to motivational speaker, Jim Rohn. But it's bigger than that. You're the average of ALL the people who are in your line of sight and sometimes you may be more influenced by strangers online than by your own family or friends. Look around and make sure you are surrounded (in real life and virtually) by people who are in line with the life you want. That's not to say you ditch people who aren't like you or striving to be better but it is being conscious of the time and energy placed on them. You don't need to flee the country and change your number, although that may be a good idea for some, but you do need to find people who can help 'expand' you rather than make your view more narrow. ('Expanders' is a term coined by Lacy Phillips of 'To Be Magnetic'.)

You have to see to believe, and, on a subconscious level, we need people of reference that we can relate to before we properly believe we can have something in our lives: *If she can do it (and she came from my county, her parents are kind of like mine and she looks a bit like me and seems a bit like me) then I can do it too!*

Social media is an amazing tool in this context because you can curate a community of people that will support your vision no matter where you are in the world.

It opens up the whole world to us if we choose and allows us to see what's possible, to strive for a bigger life or a life that brings you peace. It enables you to connect with people doing things that your soul wants to do, showing you a blueprint of what your ideal life might look like.

'Expanders' are essential if we are to manifest our biggest desires. On a neurological level, they're telling your brain, and more importantly your subconscious, that it's possible for you to also achieve. When you are wavering you can check in with them and remind yourself that what you're trying to achieve is possible. It's already been done, the path has been paved.

Over time what you want to do will change. Your list of priorities will change so your list of 'Expanders' will change too but think of them as a global cast of humans who inspire you in big or little ways. You can turn the cesspit of comparison that is social media into a moving vision board.

Set some time aside to curate who you follow online (maybe you need to do this in real life too). Delete accounts that make you feel like shit. It's that simple.

Fill your feed with humans who inspire you and make you believe you can do anything you want or compel you to grow more and strive for a fuller life. You can also follow accounts that make you laugh uncomfortably with inappropriate memes. Whatever you're into, just make sure you're in the driving seat because, whether you're aware or not, the people you follow are impacting how you feel about yourself and your ability to create the life you want.

Green-Eyed Gift

Don't be afraid that a feed full of people with the job/family/ life you want will make you feel jealous. Envy and jealousy are thought to be wrong, properly wrong! Shamefully wrong. Envy is one of the seven *deadly sins*. In the Book of Genesis, envy is said to be the motivation behind Cain murdering his brother, Abel. God had a favourite and apparently that was Abel, poor Cain lost his shit and the rest is history. Envy is, therefore, a sin deeply ingrained in human nature. In women, envy is seen as petty and bitchy, to be avoided and to be swallowed as soon as it swells up. Thou shall not covet thy neighbour's goods (or job, or husband, or extension).

There is a difference between jealousy and envy although they're regularly used interchangeably. Jealousy is when you have something and you're afraid to lose it, scared or angry at the thought of someone taking it away. Envy, on the other hand, is wanting something for yourself that someone else has. It is defined as 'a feeling of discontented or resentful longing aroused by someone else's possessions, qualities, or luck.' But this emotion when embraced, or at least examined, can be wildly revealing and very powerful, leaving a little trail of breadcrumbs, notes from your subconscious, about what you desire on a deep level and what you know you can do/have/be. Become curious and open to envy; make it your friend and your guide.

Start to see those little pangs as clues. The people you look up to and admire, the ones you envy are giving you clues about who you are on the deepest level, who you have the potential to become. They have qualities you already possess, which is why you see them. They are doing something you have the potential to do; they are living a life that you can live.

Don't feel ashamed or embarrassed about those niggles; instead, try to tap into exactly what it is about that person or their life that you want – the essence of how they live that inspires you or pisses you off (usually because you want to have a bit of it). It won't always be immediately apparent – maybe you don't want to be a personal trainer like the chick on Instagram but you long to be your own boss and have freedom over your time. You may not want a(nother) child but you're longing for the connection that you witness in someone else's life. Drill down to what you're actually missing. Follow these clues to help give you clarity. Be inspired rather than threatened by this other person's achievements, knowing that you're getting closer. Take the hint and apply it in a way that feels right for you. Copy and paste only works in Word docs.

*

Never Enough

Something happened during lockdown. When everything got quiet. Silence was everywhere and, instead of it being ominous, it was glorious. I realised that what I loved wasn't the mad rush on pasta or the endless Zoom quizzes or the lack of social interaction but the lack of comparison: *I may be off, work may be quiet, but it's the same for everyone. I am not falling behind or failing and if I am then so is everyone else!* There was immense comfort in that but it also highlighted just how much my mood, my happiness and sense of accomplishment, is tied up with others. How often I can't fully enjoy something I have if someone has something better. I'm using this language to illustrate the inner child, the baby brat, the little soul, who has learned that there is not enough to go around.

You'll hear it referred to as 'scarcity mindset', a term coined by Stephen Covey in his book *The 7 Habits of Highly Effective People*. Scarcity mentality refers to people seeing life as a finite pie, so that if one person takes a big chunk, that leaves less for the rest of us. It is basically the fear or belief that there is not enough for everyone. If someone else has something good, there's nothing left for you. They get the job, you lost it. They have a baby, now babies have run out. There is a struggle in really being able to enjoy another person's success when you're operating from a core belief that they've stolen an opportunity from you.

On a rational level you might know that's not true but deep down you can't fully revel in their progress either because it feels like it's highlighting your lack thereof. It's a race and if you're not winning, you're losing. We are taught that we must scramble and compete, we must be suspicious of those who have what we want. Operating from a place of survival rather than a place of creation.

The opposite of this mode is an 'abundance' mindset, the belief that there is plenty out there for everybody. More than enough. And the more you can celebrate others and acknowledge the infinite resources and beauty and opportunities, the more they will start to appear. As you acknowledge and ENJOY someone else's success, even if it's what you long for, especially if it's what you long for, you multiply your chances of bringing it into your life. Marianne Williamson in *A Return to Love* says, 'A person who succeeds in any area is only creating more of a possibility for others to do the same. Holding on to the thought of finite resources is a way of holding on to hell.' I don't necessarily believe that hell is a flaming shithole where we're sent by God for being assholes but it's not altogether pleasant and probably somewhere you don't want to be, fire or not.

Apart from the general stuck-ness you feel when operating from a lack mentality, it's also a scary place to be. Maybe without even realising, if your belief is that abundance is gifted to only a special few and coveted or resented by the rest, on a subconscious level you may be playing small. Afraid to really step into your power and embody that sense of abundance because it's quite a dangerous position to occupy. The assumption is that if you believe this so must everyone else, which also means no one can enjoy your successes either. Others must feel awful that you stole the pie and therefore it's safer to play it down or denigrate or sabotage.

But it's much like expanders. If you step into yourself fully and live with an abundance mindset. If you believe that you are worthy of beautiful things and a satisfying career, if you properly believe that there is enough to go around and embody that, then you will start to awaken other people to that possibility too. Without trying you will open them up and help them believe. Win, win, win.

Don't equate someone else's success to your downfall, instead see it as an opportunity for what you can accomplish. Next time, see the person, feel the twist and thank them for showing you what's possible. Pause, breath and have a chat to yourself.

So, how can we make the shift from a scarcity to an abundance mindset?

- Focus on what you have, not on what you're missing
- Get grateful-journal, 'joyride', or sit in thanks for what you already have
- Acknowledge how far you've come. 'Remember when you dreamt about what you have right now?' Try to allow yourself to enjoy the journey!
- Switch off your phone and stop looking around. What you want is not 'out there'
- Get into your body
- Exercise to feel strong and capable
- Walk in nature or water your plants!
- Meet a friend with an 'abundance mindset' – someone who will see possibilities everywhere
- Make a list of what you have to offer
- Remind yourself that win-win is an option. The story that in order for one to succeed another must fail is based on a belief system that is not real.
- Train your mind to see possibilities rather than problems. When you catch yourself being negative or assuming the worst, make the choice to shift the narrative.

Toast to Little Wins

I have often been paralysed by the notion that there's not enough to go around; that even when I'd reached my goals, I'd get nothing. Somehow, despite this underlying belief, I managed to paint a decent picture and life looked good. I got the big entertainment TV job, I had a hair ad, I did all the glossy red-carpet things and I was more miserable than I have ever been in my life. The list I'd drawn up, which had felt like the longest shot, had landed in my lap – almost without effort. I'd worked my arse off but there'd been an ease, a synchronicity, and doors had opened. It was fun until it wasn't.

My focus was always on racing ahead to the next thing as quickly as I could. I never allowed myself to sit back and enjoy any of it. The present is the only thing we have but I was fixated on what next. 'What next' suggests that now is not enough. What I have is not enough. And more of that state appears. It becomes harder to feel satisfied with where you are if you're always looking for the next hit.

Allowing yourself to take a moment to savour the little wins (and the big ones) is hugely important. Not just energetically but on a soul level. Reminding yourself to not look around and diminish your success by comparison to someone else's. Sitting with yourself and saying thanks. Well done! Thanks for taking me here. Thank you to that spark. That inner knowing that was so blindingly naive and free. Thank you for following that. For all the experiences that brought me to this moment – good and bad. Thank you.

Chapter Five

What's Broken is Beautiful

It might be your mother's fault or your ex-boyfriend's or your uncle's cousin's cat's but who gives a shit; it's holding YOU back, not them.

Taking responsibility isn't punishment, it's empowerment. It means you can start again on your own terms. When I first sat down to write this book, I thought I had nothing but sad stories and Instagram quotes. Where was the meat? I have kept a diary forever, but it's always been the same: I write to process pain; I do my best writing when I am angry or spiteful or suffering. I vomit it onto the page without thought or judgement and always feel a bit lighter afterwards. But those are the tatty old pages that no one will ever see (at least until I die and then it's grand); these are not committed to printed pages and pushed out into the world wrapped in a colourful sleeve with my name there for all to see, forever to read. What if all I have are sad, sad stories that expose my over-sensitivity and make me look indulgent and spoiled? Classic 'first world problems'.

I like to think this book isn't a bunch of sad stories. Instead, they're the moments that define me, but that I'm proud to have overcome. Little lessons I've learned that I hope might help someone else. There is a confidence and pride that comes from knowing you can survive hard things, even if they're only 'hard' in your eyes. Perception is everything and your suffering may look like a gift to one person and a load too heavy to bear when viewed through the eyes of someone else. Whatever those stories are for you, you have the power to reframe them at any time you like. The things that shake you shape you. Things that make you grow also make you great. And if you look at them as moving stories, then they are ever-changing. You see them differently every time you look, discover something new, shift with some other bit of knowledge.

We all have stories that shape who we are, that cement certain beliefs as fact, that become part of the tales we tell about ourselves. But how we view those experiences can change; *we* can change if we remain open and the scars we have can become the bits we hold dearest.

Scar Tissue

No one said it better than Leonard but it's not just a genius lyric. When we think of wounds and scars, we often think of damage. Wounds are the chinks in our armour. Gaps in our glory. Little glitches. Events, memories, traumas that have somehow weakened us just a bit (or quite a lot). We endure them; we maybe even accept them but rarely do we revel in them and cherish the wisdom they offer us.

Of course, wounds are an inevitable part of being human – not just the cuts and bruises, the little elbow scar from the neighbour's dog or the dodgy slice on your leg from jumping stone walls at the Gaeltacht. Even if your body is unmarred and shows no evidence of a life lived, mistakes made or suffering endured, you will carry emotional wounds, and these 'cracks' provide us with a chance for insight and self-discovery.

An open wound can either be viewed as something we must bandage up and hide from the world or as a glorious, tender invitation into our souls. The wound is a giant, flashing neon sign, a call for work to be done. The place where healing starts. If they are welcomed and embraced, our wounds can become the key to our freedom.

I saw them as scars to be hidden away, under clothes and strained smiles, kept in the dark where no one, not even me, could see. A wound, a hurt, an old story that catches in your throat, a memory that makes your breath short and your heart shrink. Those are the best ones. Those are the ones we most need to embrace; they are our greatest teachers. Switching them from something terrifying and shameful, something to be avoided, into something that offers a lesson (no matter how difficult) changes our relationship and allows us to approach without fear to maybe even be grateful when they show up.

When we are no longer driven by fear but by curiosity to know ourselves more fully, wounds become beautiful little keyholes with slivers of light escaping through, hoping to catch our attention, to invite us in. The most painful ones are signposts that, when followed, will lead us to our greatest discoveries or maybe they just lead us back to ourselves.

Deck the Halls

People often talk about being triggered around Christmas or whatever holiday you celebrate. The very act of going home feels triggering. Anticipating it. Packing makes you feel overwhelmed, like every pair of knickers in the case is an extra day you must survive. Home is triggering as it is very often where our little or big wounds were inflicted. Stepping through the door activates them all over again. We revert to survival mode, on edge, on high alert, ready for some sort of attack. The people who know you best offer you safety and warmth and love, but they are also the ones who know your weaknesses. They know how to push your buttons without even touching them. Their own wounds open back up just looking at you. Without doing a single thing, without any intention to cause harm or discomfort, you are activated!

As I went on my own healing journey, I kept hearing this word 'trigger' and I used it but never quite understood it. I figured that anything that sounds like it might kill you should be avoided at all costs. If I'm triggered, I need to get down quick. Hide and wait for it to blow over. Distract and wait for the coast to clear. And that's an option. The sense of being 'triggered' dissipates and things go back to normal. But what if normal is not enough or at least not what you really want any more. What if you know deep down that you want to change, that survival is no longer enough. You want to thrive; you want to soar. Triggers can become your greatest teachers and the beauty (and torture) is that they're everywhere, every day, all over the fucking place!

A Different Kind of Forest Bathing

A few months ago I was taking my daughter to nursery. She goes to a Forest School so drop-off is in the woods. No school-gate nonsense but also no actual school gate, which is fine unless you were born with a banjaxed GPS. I had given us loads of time deciding the night before that we would meander, have a chat, enjoy the journey instead of hurtling lunchbox-in-hand, late, towards the destination. So far so lovely.

We got to where I thought the camp was that day, where it had been for the last few weeks, but there was nothing. No tents, no humans, no sign of life. We kept going. I kept telling my little girl that all was fine; silly Mama got lost. I was determined to remain CHILL. It didn't really matter if we were a bit late anyway, this was a lovely experience and when else do you get to be genuinely lost in the woods with your two-year-old. BLISS, right!?

But without warning I could suddenly feel the hot flames rising in my chest, my throat tightened, my stomach lurched. 'This is an old response to something else,

Angela, but this current situation doesn't warrant panic or fury. It's 8.45am. Calm the fuck down. Love you? I was talking myself off the ledge, talking myself down, but I also wanted to show my daughter that I was absolutely fine with being lost, that we don't always have to know our way, that frustration is a valid emotion too and it's important to let that out. Did I mention it's now 8.50am? I asked strangers but no one had a clue. I was now furious with myself and my stupidity. I kept saying out loud, 'I'm so annoyed, I'm so annoyed,' just so my daughter knew my anger wasn't aimed at her. We were finding her school but it wasn't her fault.

I asked if she knew where we should go; her guess at this stage was as good as mine. Maybe her untainted intuition could help us get out of that damn forest. She then said, 'Mummy, will we just go home?', which was exactly what I wanted to do but figured it was a lesson in giving up so said no. She picked up a pigeon feather and we decided that maybe the feather could help us find the way. Annoyingly it was woeful at directions too. I was firing off emails and texts, asking other mothers and the nursery where the hell I was supposed to go, gently, passive aggressively, obviously because I was pretty sure I had fucked up and no one else. Then my kid said, 'Mama, are you still annoying?' which made me laugh and realise that this whole thing was a farce and that all I wanted was a hot whiskey and a hug. *I was annoying.* It was annoying.

Eventually, with a little more guidance from strangers and having reread an email that instructed me on exactly where to go, we found it, 90 minutes late. We were welcomed like warriors returning from battle. I was mortified; she was oblivious but also knackered after our impromptu detour. I left relieved, furious, ashamed, and completely triggered. This was not normal; there had to be some sort of life lesson in here, something I could salvage from this shitshow.

I went home and meditated. I went back to the searing heat in my chest. Where had I felt it before? When? Back and back, earlier and earlier ... I was standing in a shopping centre in Dublin city centre. We were country kids; we rarely came to 'town' so nothing was familiar; everything was enormous. I felt a million miles from home. I'm five-ish, or at least that's how I look in this image. My mam is browsing in a clothes shop. I'm messing about, touching dresses and bobbing under rails of polyester. I look around to find her and she's gone. I am in the shop and I'm on my own. I panic. I run outside the shop desperate to see her so I can run after her and she can scoop me up and ruffle my hair and we can laugh and skip off holding hands. I can't see her. She's disappeared and I'm going to be here forever in this awful shopping centre until I die, alone.

A security guard sees me. I see him and he looks official and I tell him I'm lost. And, the moment I tell him, I feel scared, because what if he's not a security guard? How is he going to find my mam anyway? He doesn't even know what she looks like? *I* can hardly remember. What if he kidnaps me? I am full of terror. I am paralysed with fear and I want to collapse. I've been forgotten; they've all gone home and they don't even realise I'm still here. They didn't even miss me. I want to cry but I don't. I try to look calm, like I'm a big, brave girl and I know she'll be back 'any minute now' just like the big dude is telling me. I can feel red-hot tears bubbling up in my tender little eyes. Then I spot her. Or she spots me! She was in the changing room; where did I go? 'Of course I wouldn't go home without you!' Kids eh?!*

That day in the woods, I felt like that little lost girl, desperate and alone, unimportant, forgotten, stupid. That day in the woods when my heart raced it wasn't because I was in danger, genuinely concerned I would never make it home, but my body didn't know that. The memory of that moment or another or a million more lodged deep in my body informed every reaction I had until awareness arrived – where I recognised that I am not that lost little girl, that I'm a grown-ass woman with Google Maps.

We are not children now; mostly we are not in danger. We have the choice then, when we start to recognise

"People and situations can trigger our mirrors to reflect back to us what we believe to be true about life, the Universe, and ourselves. Mirrors reveal the parts of us that are yet to be accepted, witnessed, or loved"

Rebecca Campbell

these 'old' feelings swelling up, to either be swept away or to stop and breathe. To take a moment in a leafy wood to reassure that little child inside you that you are safe. That you are not stupid for getting lost, you have not been forgotten, you are here now and everything is OK.

*PS I was lost in the shopping centre for all of 3–5 minutes, maybe less, but my perception in that moment is what formed that memory. My mam didn't buy the trousers she'd tried on, but I did get a lolly.

When someone or something reminds us of an unhealed experience, we get triggered. Don't walk away or cower in a corner waiting to be called for dinner! Take the opportunity to examine these triggers and what they're trying to show you. When did you feel this before? When was the first time you felt it? Can you revisit it and play it out in a different way. Reprogramming a memory that still has a visceral hold over you can be very powerful. Go back into the moment, let the emotions build up and then give yourself what you needed then. A hug from an adult, validation, defence, reassurance, maybe you just needed to be told you were loved in any given moment. Paint a picture of the reimagined event and feel those heavy emotions leave your body.

> "Yesterday's medicine has become today's poison"

Mastin Kipp

Feel the Fear and Eat It

Fear is a great and powerful, dominant, insidious, ominous little bitch! It is the single biggest thing that prevents us from living the lives we want. It keeps us safe but mostly it keeps us stuck. Often we have no idea what we're even afraid of but those shadowy plumes are everywhere – they're inside us directing us and stopping us from moving.

What are you afraid of? Start to get acquainted with your fears, make friends with them. Keeping enemies closer and all that jazz! Get to know them. We can be so afraid to engage with our fears that we have no idea what we're actually afraid of. If we admit they're there, look them in the eye, they might consume us. They might grow and swallow us whole or drown us in a minute.

Root out your fears with determination but a gentle touch. Commit to it but tread softly. For some of us, they permeate everything; everywhere we are they are too. They are stuck in your creaky knees, lodged in between the vertebrae in your back, whispering in your mouth. Hold them, feel them, get to know them. Let them percolate in your deepest crevices, roam freely around inside you. Explore them and maybe, more importantly, let them explore you. Instead of turning away, turn the plumes of dark, murky smoke into mist or vapour. Let your courage and curiosity to explore them alchemise.

Turn the stagnant energy and fearful heaviness of the unknown into light and get excited about stepping out of the shadow of your own fears because only when you've faced them will they start to dissipate. They may still hang around but they're harmless now. They can't hurt you or keep you small when you see them. That is your power, your ability to change yourself, your approach and your outlook. Change your perspective at any time you want.

It may feel safe to avoid the pain and sweep the painful memories under the shagpile rug but there is no growth in safety. Trauma, like shame, thrives in silence. Blooms in silence. The longer you starve it of light and oxygen the deeper inside it will go. The fear of really seeing it can be paralysing. Once you see it you can't unsee it so there must be a real willingness to open to the truth and to say goodbye to what you knew. Most of us are not ready to say goodbye even if we're being smothered where we are.

When you sit in your body and fully surrender, to fully ADMIT the truth of your experience without fear of the consequences, you can start to live. On your own terms,

"I am grateful for all the lessons that have led me here . . . It doesn't mean I don't have tough days – it means I lean into tough days with curiosity and courage"

Makenzie Marzluff

freely. You don't have to be driven by survival any more; you can give yourself the things you needed, the things you never got. You can start to rewrite your past and recreate your future. You can see your past clearly, thank it for taking you to this moment right here and know that you are exactly where you're supposed to be. Exactly as you are. You don't need to be afraid.

Fear is not to be feared; pain is not to be fled – embrace it like an acquaintance you half like. You're not 100% convinced on the motives but you quite like the shoes.

Stay open to what you might discover about yourself and your behaviour. Study yourself and start to dismantle the ridiculous thoughts and beliefs you have that are born out of fears that are built on shaky ground. Investigate your fears and beliefs like a child on the brink, knowing that you're about to be all grown up. Open your glorious mind to the possibility of living in freedom without these dipshits steering the ship.

"For as long as I can remember, I have felt disconnected from things and people. There have, of course, been moments of bliss and love but usually fear is hovering close by waiting for an in. The beautiful states of being aren't allowed to last very long. I am not allowed to blossom or flourish. The dogged master watching me and waiting to pounce is dressed like me. The threat is not outside; it lives within. The cure is not outside; it also lives within"

Me!

Deliciously Salty Truth

While I was off doing 'the work', self-reflection/exploration was something I took very seriously. No days off. The same intensity that's applied to most things I do was directed towards 'healing'. I followed all the accounts, read psychology books, did therapy, I was mainlining alternative therapies too like a junkie – all in the hope that I could nail this thing called life and hopefully learn how to live better. I was immensely proud of how far I had come but most of my experiences were in a vacuum. I obsessively worked in hiding with the view to re-emerging like a goddess.

So, the first time I came home for Christmas after this period was a bit of a kick in the arse. I was shocked to find that nothing had really changed at all. I imagined I would be met with applause. I figured they would see my radiant aura and the peace emanating from me. I had been healing my wounds FFS. But nothing. Maybe I should have shaved my head or worn an orange cloak. I presumed I would suddenly have the right words to express myself. I would lead healing circles and we would drink cacao at the winter solstice! Instead, my dad lit a bonfire (accidentally) on the 21st, we danced with the kids on top of a heap of muck in wet rain on half-dug foundations. We sang to Florence Welch and we howled like wolves. Accidentally.

I was pushing myself to be better, determined not to revert to my sulky teenage ways. Determined not to revert to all the behaviours that I seem to so easily slip back into, despite my best intentions. I needed a drink. That night, there were margaritas in my sister's new house, margaritas with an edge of words unspoken. I could feel the tension but couldn't articulate a thing. I felt unwanted and overlooked – common themes but felt more deeply since I naively thought I was my own little zen island. I had levitated above those needs for validation and acceptance!

I thought I was ready to talk. To connect. To forgive. I was pumped! What I hadn't accounted for was the possibility that while I was off excavating my own history so were the rest. When my revelations and bitter accusations were met with resistance and anger, I buckled. I realised for the first time that the hurt I felt may also have been dealt by me. Wounds felt by others but this time with me wielding the knife (this was not how it ended in my head). I had spent so long wrapped up in my own experience, reliving, unpicking, reframing all the little things (and big things) that had shaped me and my belief system, that the idea that others may have been deeply hurt by me and my actions or attitudes, hadn't even occurred to me. I was utterly unique in my suffering. Until I wasn't.

The upside of this was that the relief I was so desperately seeking came from a different place. It wasn't an eloquent and dramatic apology, the kind that you quote and frame on a wall. It was a booze-fuelled, heated, and heavy discussion that went up and down and around in circles. One filled with anger and frustration, blame and love. Like a silent disco – both madly dancing, trying to connect but listening to different tunes, never quite in sync. Turning towards someone just as they turned away, turning away just as they leaned in.

It was then that I realised that we're all hurting to a greater or lesser extent; we are dealing with things old and new, cuts that are fresh and open – the kind that require immediate attention ... all hands on deck. They are visible and painful to witness even if they're not your own. And then there are deep, dormant wounds that are so old, so woven into the fabric of your family, so often discussed and familiar in their quiet presence that they are presumed benign. Until you've had some margaritas.

The healing I got that night was not from a one-sided apology, the kind I arrogantly expected; it came from a realisation that that might never come. And that was OK. I saw the hurt I had caused too, ways I had disconnected and disappeared. In attempting to heal myself, I had retreated, never really considering the impact, too wrapped up in my own process. The healing I got was born out of a shared desire to make things better. To press reset. To clear the air and start all over again but I needed to accept where I was now. Although not at all as I imagined there was comfort in knowing that I could bare my teeth, let my searing pent-up anger spill out unedited, sloppy, careless, and still be loved . . . That the 'conclusion' I was after would only ever come if the story was over, and it never is.

It is easy to be grateful for the good stuff when things are going well, but growth and peace come when we welcome in the hard stuff just the same. Tolerating the messy painful truths that live within ourselves and our homes. When we can dance into the situations and wounds that make us feel most vulnerable and find something of value. When we can walk into the flames and know that the burn will also offer us something. It's hard to trust that in a moment of pain there might also be love but that's where the magic happens. You can start to get excited about the prospect of growth and lessons in every day; a deeper understanding of yourself is the payoff for standing in the flames. A deeper connection with yourself and an ability to connect more deeply with those around you too. A quiet, beautiful, messy place of truth. Just not for Instagram.

Chapter Six

Welcoming a Crowd of Sorrows

've had a love/hate relationship with death for as long as I can remember. It excites me. As a kid it felt dangerous to discuss and so I would bring it up whenever I could, at the most inappropriate times. I would daydream about my own funeral – the music and the heartbreak of all those I had left behind. Dying felt like an act of rebellion. Like two fingers to anyone who had ever mistreated me or overlooked me. They'd be sorry now, I'd think. I still say it now as a joke to my husband: 'you'll miss me when I'm dead' – it's shocking and surprising but also serves as a reminder to come back to now, to find some perspective. You'll be sorry when I'm dead.

The drama of a funeral has always been wildly appealing to me. The sense of theatre. The plumes of frankincense, the velvet robes and satin-lined boxes. The idea that the mourners are on stage, part of some sort of amateur production. But I think my fondness for funerals came from the intimacy that perhaps wasn't there day to day. At funerals everyone hugged; it wasn't weird or weak to cry, to feel broken or vulnerable. It was welcomed. You shook hands with people you didn't know and felt their skin and smelled their smells. You were held by strangers and people looked in your eyes – you said sorry or they did but there was a moment of connection that felt special, almost illicit.

At the house there were sandwiches and singing, stories and fizzy drinks. You could stay up late and watch your parents not be parents. You would see them as real-life people, not just your designated minders. This was both thrilling and terrifying.

The Day That Dolly Died

The first time I realised my mam was a human and not just my mother was when I was seven years old and Margaret Murray collected us from school in the old navy estate car that felt long like the legs of her delightfully lanky children. They were oddly exotic and so was that dusty old car with plant pots and muck and garden tools. She wasn't supposed to pick us up; it was Mam's turn. It was also early. We all left school. There was a quick stop off at the church and then straight to Macentaggarts! They sold footballs alongside school uniforms and tyres, wellies, Mars bars and sweeping brushes. We needed new clothes apparently. All very strange. I didn't know at the time but my intuition could smell a rat and all this distraction with sweets and new cardigans was not doing it for me.

'Your granny is dead.' Like a slap in the face. I smiled or cried; I actually don't remember. I just felt guilty, immediately. A feeling that would become more familiar and more persistent as the years rolled on. I felt guilty. I hadn't killed her so it didn't make sense. Maybe I had killed her? I didn't hug her much last time she visited. I wouldn't walk up the cul-de-sac with her because William Smith was up there and she wasn't 'cool'. Maybe I broke her heart. I did. I broke her heart when I laughed at the way she said 'vexed'. When I would run away from her, knowing she couldn't catch me. It was cruel. I was cruel and my cruelty killed her.

It didn't. She died in her sleep. A sudden heart attack. Just like her husband . . . years before and her son . . . years after. 'A good way to go'; 'no suffering'; 'harder for the ones left behind, but she was lucky'. The door opened and I could tell my mam didn't think that Granny was lucky; that she didn't feel lucky herself.

We were on the porch. The odd excitement of a change in routine starting to shift into hollow reality. Her eyes were raw, tears rolling down her reddened cheeks, her face like a broken plate.

She was a child who had lost her mother. I realised she was a little girl too, just like me. She was scared too, just like me.

That day on that porch my life changed; it changed my mam. She was 37 and had four little girls. I could feel her grief like a molten rock in my stomach, like a fizzing panicked choking in my throat. When my granny stopped breathing, we all held our breath. Our solid ground shaken, our foundations rattled, trust in the grown-ups' endurance suddenly gone.

We got in the car – I don't remember whose – and were in Galway in a few hours. The 'hairy road', so-called because of the tufty green landing strip leading all the way to her house, was usually the route to freedom, a cupboard full of sweets, heaped boiled buttery potatoes, apple tart, herding cows and driving a tractor before you could properly drive a tricycle. It was loose and wild and safe. Until it wasn't. I could smell her as soon as we walked in. Talc and Oil of Ulay. She was in her bedroom, laid out in the bed. The peach quilt that would live in our house for years to come covering her cold feet. I missed her already but at least she was still here. I wish I'd known her more. I wish she knew me now.

The range was on and the house was busy with people preparing for the crowds later. We scurried around as people we never met offered sympathy we didn't deserve. Sandwiches being made, drinks being poured, tears being shed – but this was the business bit. The busyness was a distraction from the reality of her abandonment. I climbed onto her bed; she was dead but she just looked asleep. Wasn't I so cute and so brave, 'not one bit afraid', except I was. I touched her cold hands and rubbed my face to her papery skin; she was fab. Why didn't I tell her while she was alive? Why didn't I hug her every single time I could and bring her up the cul-de-sac and show her off to all my friends. She was wonderful. And it was too late to tell her. I understood now why my mam's heart was broken.

My dad was silently there, keeping the show on the road: serving drinks and sorting parking; making sure things were paid for, and holding his head. A steady presence. He loved Dolly. And she loved him too, enough to hand over her only daughter to him a few months after losing her husband. She knew a good egg when she met one; she trusted him to hold my mother. He held her physically as she sobbed. He held Granny now. The coffin on his shoulders, helped by her two sons, and some neighbours, I suppose. People did readings. My older sister was always good at those although she hated it. I closed my eyes and breathed in the frankincense, the plumes of smoke soothing my frighted little soul. I liked funerals because the theatrics distracted me from the pain and fear and loss (imagined, anticipated or real). The everydayness of grief was briefly forgotten in the ceremony. Distracting me from the overwhelming weight, a weight I was sure I couldn't bear.

Premature Ageing (of a different kind)

For many people losing someone close can be a new beginning. I have interviewed many guests on my chat show and podcast 'Thanks A Million' who've made peace with the loss of a parent at a young age. People who managed to find the silver lining in a devastating loss or who used it as a catalyst to change their path. It used to sound a bit shocking to me, heartless even. But that experience up close, being confronted with your own mortality, can break you or fuel you. Many people talk about how life changes after a near-death experience. So whether it's your own head-on collision with the next life or whether you held the hand of someone passing over themselves, there is no escape. Everything you thought you know comes into sharp focus.

Perhaps the loss of a parent makes you grow up quickly, forces you into adulthood. Pushes you to walk even if you don't feel quite ready or you were really hoping to crawl for a bit longer. I remember after I got married being sent away on honeymoon, waved off by my family with some petals and a warning to go quick in case we missed the flight. I felt like I had been handed over, cast out, thrown from the nest. I was 33, I had just married the love of my life, I was happy, but it still knocked me sideways.

I was a 'fully-fledged adult'. You're probably one too. We have adult bodies, adult responsibilities, adult careers, we make adult decisions every day. But I think I'm not alone in saying I often feel like I'm playing at being a grown-up. Constantly waiting for the parent to arrive, cook me dinner and tuck me in. To save me from myself and take control again.

I am secretly searching for approval from anyone who cares. *'Is this right? Are you OK with this? Will you still love me? Will you look after me if it all goes tits up?'* We are afraid to take full responsibility not just because it falls with us when things don't take perfect shape or when we falter, as we will. But I think we're also afraid to give ourselves permission to shine, to BLOSSOM fully, to show up powerfully. We are waiting for someone to come along and tell us we're fabulous and that it's time to get out there and show them all. But that person isn't coming to usher you onto the stage, and maybe with loss you recognise this sooner. You realise you are the one that needs to nudge yourself gently (or not) into the light. Into your own light.

In a way, the pandemic has given us a collective shake. Not just the appalling losses people have endured, but the time to reassess. Without the noise and distraction of life, without shiny things and hectic schedules, places to go, people to see. That all ground to a halt and the silence was ringing in our ears. A collective grief for a life we knew and the freedoms we took for granted. A grief for the state of the world. A time to sigh loudly. To sit quietly. To ask the questions that we often avoid until they slap us in the face through a dramatic event or loss. What am I doing? Is this it? Even asking those questions is risky because they will be answered whether you like those answers or not. EAT. SLEEP. DRINK. BUY. SCROLL. REPEAT. It's safer.

But safety is not what we came here for. Actually, safety is lovely but the comfort that is a familiar blanket can also be a dead weight. Looking at yourself in the mirror and asking, 'who do I want to be?' What the hell do you want to do and then finding a way to do it. People who have seen death up close or who have come close themselves are often free of the fears that hold so many of us back.

My dad used to always say, 'Go for it, you could be dead tomorrow', which, as a teenager, felt a bit bleak and not altogether plausible, but it has become a life motto for me even if it makes me laugh every time I think it: 'you could be dead tomorrow'; you could. I hope you're not and I hope we live to be grey and wrinkly and bursting with wisdom and wit but we *could* be dead tomorrow. What would you do today if you thought you'd be gone tomorrow? Who would you hug? Would you start a business or go back to school, quit your job and follow love? What are you waiting for? Don't put your life on pause because you worry about what dickheads you'll never meet think. Free yourself from the belief that we have forever and start to live with a boldness that comes when there's no going back. That is the energy we're going for.

List the Things you Might Do if Tomorrow was the End . . .

Who are you waiting for?

Are you wasting time? Or filling it with noise while neglecting the seemingly ordinary things that feed you?

Revisit the dreams you had as a child; can you reintroduce things that nourish you?

WHAT are you waiting for?

*

"The difference between those people 'living their potential' and those who don't, is not the amount of potential itself, but the amount of permission they give themselves to live in the present"

Marianne Williamson

Love Out Loud

How often do you think, 'God, I love her', or 'I must tell him just how much he means to me' or 'I admire that person so much'?! Maybe you say it in your head, but the person never hears and then it loses its intensity and the moment passes. You write a text or email or letter, you pick up the phone, but you stop. You think I should, I must, I will . . . tomorrow. And tomorrow turns into next week, then next year, things change; life gets in the way or maybe that person is no longer here. I lost a friend a couple of years back. We were due to meet at Christmas and we never did; it stings even now and although seeing him wouldn't have changed anything, I really wish I had. What are you waiting for? Tell the people you love how much you LOVE them NOW; let it spill out of you all messy, over the top, ineloquent; be the annoying one in your WhatsApp group!

Love, not to get it back, but because to hold it in is harder than to let it flow.

The Guest House

By Rumi

This being human is a guest house.
Every morning a new arrival.

A joy, a depression, a meanness,
some momentary awareness comes
as an unexpected visitor.

Welcome and entertain them all!
Even if they're a crowd of sorrows,
who violently sweep your house
empty of its furniture,
still, treat each guest honourably.
He may be clearing you out
for some new delight.
The dark thought, the shame, the malice,
meet them at the door laughing,
and invite them in.

Be grateful for whoever comes,
because each has been sent
as a guide from beyond.

Welcome Them All

Feeling 'good' is not my default setting. It was not inherited, or perhaps it was but I gave it back! Optimism, happiness, and positivity eluded me for a very long time, which is often surprising to people who know me but don't KNOW me. I have learned to access these feelings more easily but it's something I have to work on constantly. We're conditioned from day dot to identify feelings as either positive or negative, and stick them in boxes accordingly – welcoming some and shunning others . . .

From the time we're babies, or certainly toddlers, we learn to control our emotions, recognising them as good or bad. Anything painful, messy, snotty, difficult, uncomfortable should be shut down, dismissed in the relentless pursuit of happiness.

Being friendly? Fine. Being moody? Not cool. Being happy, great. Sad? Boring. Needy? Inconvenient. Compliant: ideal. Angry: unacceptable. I think this expectation to live in positive emotions and deny the messier more challenging ones is particularly relevant for women. We are taught to present as passive, smiling, easy, helpful, happy, 'good little girls'. Don't rock the boat. Don't shout or scream, don't hit or demand, be quiet and lovely and pretty. And please shut up. Good girl.

Most of us learn to put these emotions into different compartments and deny half of ourselves in the process. In theory this isn't a major problem. We should be 'thinking positive'; think negatively and you'll attract more of that into your life, that's the drill. On the surface that appears to work, but those 'nasty' uncomfortable feelings don't go anywhere except deeper inside. The emotions that you reject as unacceptable are swallowed and sit in your being like lead weighing you down or lava ready to explode.

The thing is, in the relentless pursuit of happiness, we minimise the importance and value of a whole spectrum of emotions. What if we're supposed to FEEL feelings. All of them. What if happiness is not the ultimate goal but, instead, deep connection to every feeling and colour. This initially struck me as radical – that the 'bad' ones might be just as valid as the 'good' – until I realised that I couldn't feel much of either. I was 'comfortably numb'. The truth is, if you turn down the dial on the messy stuff, you deny yourself the rest. If you numb yourself to pain, you also tap out of pleasure. If you refuse to sit with the discomfort, you will never know peace.

Often our absolute refusal to feel the heavy emotions stems from a deep fear that we will buckle under their weight. That we will be engulfed by their intensity, their enormity. But if you can allow yourself to melt into them, let them pour over you and know that they are on you not in you, they are not you. You are experiencing them. They are passing. Then, you can let them wash over you, pass by, watching them but not becoming them.

Now, I try to embrace anger and pain, guilt, fear, all the juicy ones. They come at inconvenient times. It annoys me that I can't simply ignore them, that I am not super-human. I am human . . . and I remind myself that 'human' is not 'average' or 'unremarkable' or 'unspecial', if that's even a word. The opposite of human is not 'superhuman'; it is inhuman. Robotic. Unfeeling. Hard. Cold. To expect our-selves to operate as robots denies us the joyful and glorious messiness of living as a human.

Embracing the full spectrum with a sense of curios-ity rather than fear means we can open ourselves up to learning rather than shut off to protect ourselves. We can welcome them all with thanks, anticipating the lessons they might bring. Where has this feeling come from? What can it teach me? How can I grow? If you properly lean into this approach, it's almost exciting to be met with a feeling of despair or disgust or jealousy. Because if you use it rather than swallow it, you can not only learn something about yourself but also be assured that the upside will be sweeter than ever.

By *feeling* pain, really feeling it with every fibre rather than fighting it from a place of fear, it will pass more quickly, without resistance, and the lighter more 'acceptable' feelings will be so much fuller and more colourful. You will feel connection and deep happiness at simple things you never really noticed before. You will feel relief and gratitude that the pain has passed. You will feel pride that you endured and survived, even thrived. You will feel confident that you can bear those feelings. That you are strong. Stronger than you know.

Powerwash

Today took me out and not in a cute way – no heels, no babysitter. It reared up like a wild beast and wouldn't relent. I wanted to run. To the fridge, to my phone, back to work, back to bed. Away. Away from the swelling tightness in my chest. The throbbing worry I couldn't locate. The bubbling panic. I wanted to swallow it but it came. So today I let it.

When I was a kid I had a tape recorder (yes, I'm one hundred and five!) and I used to take it to bed and play Elvis's 'Only Fools Rush In' and weep. I think of this often and, although it sounds woefully pathetic, it was a bit lovely. So I played some sad music. I filled my ears with Elvis and Ludovico Einaudi.

I followed the waves, the heights and the crashes and allowed myself to fold into it. I sat against the wall in my bedroom, a blanket wrapped around me, and I cried. Deep, wet, angry, ugly sobs. You know the kind. I cried for myself and the little me, I cried for you! I cried for everyone; for things they might not even cry about themselves. I wept and it was perfect. Cathartic.

Often, the fear with letting the dam open is that you'll drown, that you will buckle under the force of this pressure and never re-emerge, but the truth is you won't. You'll struggle under the weight and thrash about for a bit, fight it. But when you know you won't die and that it will pass, you can relax into it. Let the weight envelop you and wrap you and throw you about a bit like a toddler with a toy. A loving kind of rattle. You can taste the salty tears and open your eyes briefly to see flowers sent by a friend and a picture you love. You can even smile and marvel at how these two bits of you, these two emotions, can live alongside each other . . . can inhabit the same space, the same second. You turn up the music and lie back and let it take you completely. This too shall pass.

The Pull

You can have good things and still miss things, I find. You can surrender and still wonder about the things that didn't happen. Still feel the disappointments; actually, you've got to. Feel them ALL, at the same time; it's a trip.

I hate missing. The pain of it weighs on me before the separation even starts. Missing comes loaded with feelings of guilt, of not being there enough, not being here enough, not being enough enough.

To acknowledge that I will miss things and humans makes me unbearably sad. I feel like I will die. Like the separation will rob me of air and food and I will cease to be. Relationships cannot survive separation. *I* cannot survive separation. I miss everything. I miss people when they're beside me. So I stop and I squash (this is not an approach I recommend). In autopilot, I begin to detach days before the separation; if I can help it, I will never attach to begin with. It is less painful. Except it's not.

The pain I feel at leaving (for work or drinks or a trip around the world) is worsened by the fact that connection hasn't really been made. Those moments of togetherness that feed a relationship long after you've physically gone are lost when you're always halfway out the door. It may feel less painful as you wave goodbye but the emptiness is worse.

There is sustenance in your thoughts and shared memories, in your seemingly mundane moments of intimacy. There is value in opening your heart fully every day you can, every minute of every day. There is joy and comfort in knowing you were there fully and completely and that you have something special enough to miss. The pull of someone far away or close but sleeping by the time you get home.

Missing someone is proof of good work, time spent nurturing, lives intertwined. The gift of missing comes with love. It is a receipt, part of the transaction. Not a price but proof. It is a privilege to love and be loved so deeply that your bones ache at the thought of separation. It is also inconvenient when there's an Addison Lee outside and a train to catch.

But you can leave knowing you'll survive the missing when you're gone, if you've fed the union while you were home. Be present and grateful in the moments when you are with people, no matter how vulnerable it may feel.

Sometimes doing the hard thing means you don't take anything for granted. When you can make it home on time, you will look in her eyes not at your phone, you will kiss him and thank him for eggs on toast and a glass of wine.

You will remember how close you were to not sharing that moment, but you only know how precious these are when you haven't made them all.

When you have cried in the back of a car because your heart aches and all you want is to wrap her in fresh pyjamas and casually kiss her goodnight with a ruffle on her head and a knowing that you'll be there when she wakes. Except you won't so you sneak in while she's asleep and you sit on her bed and you stroke her sweet little face, secretly hoping she might wake just for long enough to look into your eyes and into your soul! Just long enough for her to know that she is held in every moment, no matter where you are or how busy you may seem.

She is there and you are now, but you tell her that all she has to do is think of you whenever and you're with her, except this is a little abstract for a two-year-old so she takes her bunny and snuggles him tight. She knows you're right there and she feels you when you're not.

The gift of missing, of allowing yourself to feel it so deeply is that you are alive and present when you get home.

'Cause you Gotta Have Faith

What will be will be. What's for you won't pass you. When your number is up, it's up!

These were sayings I grew up hearing but heartily eye-rolled at. Actually, it often angered me. My mam telling me that the way life panned out had nothing to do with me (at least that's what I heard) made me furious. It was such an easy, passive thing to say. It took away accountability, but it also took away opportunity. It suggested to me that you just strap in and hope for the best. That you are a passenger in a life that's predetermined. I hated that and I hated her a little for delivering it as fact.

I would win and succeed and work and triumph no matter what 'God' had in mind. I would beat the system. What I hadn't realised was that I was assuming he had feeble plans for me. I was assuming that his ambition for me was less than my own. Less exciting and less extraordinary.

Over the years I have taken this message delivered in more palatable ways from the mouths of strangers. Go with the flow. Accept. Surrender. Lean in, lean out, shake it all about. I heard these words and began to feel their power.

I had rejected God as some sort of dominant monster in the sky, writing life plans for people he never consulted. His work carried out by tyrannical hypocrites preaching from gilded pulpits on a Sunday while carrying out ungodly deeds the rest of the week. Their holy iron fists strangling us slowly. The extracurricular activities of a few haunted my country for generations, vivid nightmares we're still trying to wake up from. Horrors swept under carpets paid for by people with nothing and everything to lose. Without formal education, scared of 'burning in hell', rejecting their own in favour of this well-dressed dictator who collected money in a basket to ensure their rightful passage into Heaven. Money that should have been used to soothe the souls it tortured.

Well, it wasn't for me so I walked away. I went to mass when I had to, to keep the peace and show my face at Christmas. I dismissed out of hand the idea of a God with a beard and a staff and a three-day blackout. He was not my guy. And anything to do with him felt old-fashioned, outdated, ill-gotten. It also felt naive. I was much more worldly and God didn't really fit with my image.

When I got married I wanted a chic, stylish, 'loose' wedding: dancing, celebration, joy and love … I wasn't fussed on Holy Communion. We wanted a wedding that represented us as a couple, something that felt a little rebellious but also pure and inclusive. It couldn't be in a church, that wasn't the vibe. Pinterest threw up pictures of meadow weddings, floral confetti, dancing under the stars – bountiful and abundant. This was not what I saw when I closed my eyes and imagined a traditional Irish Catholic church. It wasn't what I felt either when I walked into those places of worship. Humanist, maybe? Registry office and a party? Anything but what I knew.

I consistently cited mine and my husband's parents as reasons why we might need to 'nod to Catholicism'. A prayer of the faithful here, some gifts there, Glory Be. Just to keep everyone else happy. But sometimes the traditions we are brought up with are in our bones, deeper ingrained than we might like to admit, the grip of them tighter than is comfortable; you might feel like you've outgrown it or closed the door but it's hard to fully shake the cloak of it.

I realised one day that when it comes to death, in particular, I have a very powerful tie to these traditions. Inherited or ingrained, I feel a deep connection to the rituals that surround death. The wakes but also the ceremony. I heard myself saying that I wanted the incense and people bawling as my body is lowered down, flowers and muck thrown in on top. I wanted the readings and the man in a dress and the silk-lined coffin on shaking shoulders. I wanted all the comfort of being dead and having somewhere to go and, although it didn't register at the time, that comfort was my faith. The absolute knowingness that I was going home.

How could I want those things when I'm dead but dismiss them without value when I am very much alive? How can I know deep in my soul that there is something much greater than me but feel so disgusted and dismissive at the same time? Ireland's history with the Catholic Church has meant that many people of my generation have abandoned God or at least the God they grew up fearing. The man with the flame on the kitchen wall, the constant, clawing hum of disapproval, this ominous presence aware of your every move – like Santa but all-year-round and without the promise of a gift, just Hell if you messed it up. We watched the news when abuse scandals broke in the Church and saw our own parents grapple, questioning the faith that had been bequeathed. The Mother and Baby Homes scandal; Repeal the Eighth; our trust in a system – that had never really served us anyway – shattering.

But part of the problem with things crumbling – even when they're long past their sell-by date and their dismantling is overdue – is that unless we have something else to look to, we can feel at sea. Flailing around for something to hold onto. Better the devil you know than the devil you don't.

Even if you've walked away from the church, it's hard to shake the guilt cloak, and even harder to release the heavy sense of shared responsibility. Those feelings are HEAVY and complex. The collective mourning for the people who never made it, the relief that it wasn't us, the gushing tears and red, red rage. God is supposed to protect us and keep us safe. Men and women 'of the cloth' are his chosen ones – they're supposed to give unconditionally, show us how to live better, act as guiding lights. But the lights went out and the grief is still being felt. And worse: we wonder if somehow we've been complicit: pick-and-mix religion; a traditional wedding for a good day out; a school that's down the road; Holy Communion because it's easier than making a statement or you just don't care enough to be seen to go the other way.

Religion imposes so many rules that it can be hard to trust your own compass. When you free yourself from all the rules you think you should live by and the conditions you must adhere to, you can live the way that is right for you and your family. Religion is just some shit-hot marketing wrapped around the universal thing that is LOVE. You can dress it up, kneel yourself down, spend a lifetime praying, recite the books off by heart or you can choose to live in love. To courageously drop all the rules and all of the judgements and choose to see only love and to attempt to live only in love. That is freedom.

In the end I got married, twice actually (to the same man), with two different priests. One who taught my husband at school and one who taught me how to drink Jack Daniels. The first one in front of just our parents and our two friends who introduced us. It was one of the most special, intimate and beautiful days of my life. Then ... again ... a week later, we went big. I had the dress (skirt actually), the flowers, table plans and a little page boy with a baby-blue blazer and chickenpox. My mother-in-law's friend played Luke Kelly on the flute as I walked (actually sprinted) down the aisle with my dad. I was giddy and full. Fr Paul chatted about the good old days, my sister read a poem, our cousins did readings and it was perfect. It was sacred and it was that way because we were lucky enough to find a man who was happy to honour what we wanted on our day. Not to force some list of old rules down our throats.

It was the most idyllic day ever. We married outside, drank outside and danced outside. It was us, under a canopy of trees in a woodland with friends and family sat on benches slightly bemused but also bursting. The sun dappled through. Birds singing. Babies mooching about. After our vows, we sat down and held hands and looked at each other in disbelief, how lucky are we in this moment; no matter what happens, we will always have that pure moment of love witnessed by the ones we love ... to have and to hold, till death do us part.

Chapter Seven

Live by Design, Not by Default

"Everything you
want you have

Everything you
need you have

The whole world
and all its infinite
possibilities reside
in you"

Me!

The 'M' Word

Manifestation. A loaded old word. Viral on social media. Loved by spiritual nuts and bedroom billionaires alike. It's a term that's casually thrown around a lot so we all think we know about it but it's a bit slippery to actually grab hold of. People who manage to do it are given unicorn status, assumed to have magical powers or witchy genes, but manifesting is something we can all get on board with if we can simultaneously allow for some freewheeling. We need to learn to let go – of control, old beliefs and limiting ideas about 'the way things are'.

Manifesting is essentially creating your life, by design not default. We're doing it anyway so why not be aware! Deliberate creation is consciously giving space to really think about how you would love to live. It's easy to believe that it just is, that wherever you are is where you'll always be, but you have endless power that you can tap into at any time.

I have always, always read 'self-help' books, now called 'self-development', I wasn't bothered with fiction. I wanted reading to teach me things, to help me. Through these books I became fascinated by the idea that we can change our lives, that we can use our minds, control our thoughts and choose a new course. Even just reading them felt hopeful; I felt lighter.

Enter *The Secret*! The book that took the world by storm and shoved manifesting right under our noses, impossible to escape. It was like a foreign language, but I was pretty stuck at the time and was open to trying anything. *The Secret* first introduced me to 'the law of attraction'. At this point I was mid-twenties, just out of a long-term relationship, living with my sister. I was working at a stall selling jewellery I found in charity shops and working as an assistant to a personal shopper part-time. It felt creative, but I was broke and lonely and desperate to reach a different state of mind. I felt completely lost and unsure about what it was I wanted to do with my life but I knew on a deeper level that I was meant to be doing something bigger and exciting. I could picture myself in that future life but I had no idea how to actually get there and that not knowing was driving me mad.

Those books taught me that the route is less important than a clear vision of the destination. I had that. But now I started to do it deliberately. I didn't stick a million-pound cheque on the ceiling but I started dabbling with vision boards, scrap books filled with cut-outs of the life I wanted. It focused my mind and gave me something to aim for. I would spend my commute actively painting this picture, daydreaming about a life that felt wildly removed from where I was at that time but somewhere I knew I was headed.

As time went on and small manifestations started to appear in my life, I went bigger, it felt like a game. Deliberately designing. I imagined myself in vivid detail being interviewed on *The Late Late Show*. I knew what I was wearing; I imagined what I would be asked and how I'd respond, I could feel the nerves and excitement . . . I figured there was nothing to lose.

Think

The brain doesn't know the difference between what's real and what's imagined. So our brains can affect our physiology (negatively and positively) without any physical input. Imagine a lemon. Think about the bitterness, the juiciness; think of it touching your tongue; squeeze it. Maybe you'll even start to salivate a bit! The brain doesn't know that it's in your mind so it can transport your body, helping you to experience incredible things, or chucking you back to unbearable situations. You have the power to create your own reality – with or without lemons.

So, your only job is to forget everything you've learned, lift yourself out of your current situation and start to spend time in your future. All in your mind. The limitations you have applied forever and the restrictions you've built up around yourself, the rules about how life works and what's possible – ditch them. Suspend all ideas about who you are right now in this body. Forget what your reality is in this moment, in this environment and let yourself move into the future. Now, I know I bang on about staying in the present moment and I'm into that but, when it comes to manifesting, you need to get freaky with the future. To delve in so deep that the lines between now and then blur to nothing.

Most people create from a state of being that's connected to the past. You get up every morning and fall back into the same mood. You brush your teeth the same way, take the same route to work, forget to remember to pay that bill. Copy and paste. Same actions, same feelings, same results and around and around we go. It might not be wildly enjoyable, it may not be what you signed up for, but without conscious awareness you are creating it. You are craving what Dr Joe Dispenza refers to as 'the predictable future', the comfort and ease that comes with hitting repeat on everything, going into autopilot, falling back into routine. It's not thrilling but the repetitive nature keeps you safe; it eliminates fear and shuts down any possibility of you venturing into the unknown.

Except that the unknown is delicious and you're missing out if you stay stuck. You're missing out on experience and growth, failure, connection, resilience and joy. ALL the good shit. In order to change, you've got to *actively* choose every thought you have, replacing the old, patterned ones with conscious thoughts that align with the fullest version of the life you want to live, which sounds exhausting but so is living half a life. Unless you're intercepting the recurring thoughts, the automatic responses, the historic feelings, you will continue to be a passive participant in your own life rather than the driving force. Now, before you lose your mind, don't think that every single thought you have (good or bad) can change your life (we're not that powerful) but it's more about changing your habits, rewiring your brain – steadily, repetitively, consistently.

So, who do you want to be? In an ideal world, without limitations or rules, who do you long to be?

> "I'm nothin' fancy in a world drippin' in gold But a beautiful jewel never bought, never sold"

Imelda May, *'Home'*

Dream Woman

Build your dream woman.

    Find her.

    Remember her.

    Unlock her.

    Fall in love with her.

    She is already in you.

    Take some time to sit down and daydream. I mean properly daydream about the human you want to be. It's meditation but that word can throw people off. Sitting with a plan or an intention, lingering on an image of the life you would love to live. Don't just write it down (although this helps from a subconscious point of view), picture it and feel it too. The feeling is the key but the visual is a way to get you there so go wild with a vision board if that works for you.

    If you think you can't visualise, or assume that you're not a visual person, that's nonsense. What does your kitchen look like? Imagine standing in it right now. Boil the kettle and grab your favourite mug, pour some milk, chuck the spoon in the sink. You've just made a cup of tea and are probably dribbling at the thought of the biscuit. You get the picture; you're there, you're standing in your kitchen, now get out of it and pop yourself into your dream life. Maybe it's a kitchen island, maybe it's an actual island. Start to build a detailed picture of what it feels like to be exactly where you want to be.

Maybe the sun is shining; start to feel the warmth on your skin. Ask questions so that your brain can fire up and start to create answers. What do you want your future to look and feel like? It's a question many of us never really ask so we're copying and pasting yesterday into today. Maybe we're expecting something miraculous to happen, something dramatic to change but without asking some fundamental, often uncomfortable questions, we can't even begin to imagine there's another way. But that's all you have to do right now: imagine with such technicolour clarity that your body is already in that future experience.

Feel

Really *feel* it. Give your body a taste of the future. What are you wearing? What can you see? Who are you with? How does your body feel? How do you walk, move, hold yourself? How do you FEEL? TRY IT ON.

When you start to really connect with and *remember* your future (by drawing a picture in your mind that's so real your body feels like it's actually happening), biologically it is exactly the same as remembering the past. It triggers positive feelings and memories and draws more of those types of experiences into your life. If thoughts and feelings about the past drag you back into doing the same old things and draw the same things into your life over and over again, then by stepping into your future you can choose to draw something new, something of your own making. You can create it rather than inherit it, deliberately moving from a state of survival to a state of creation.

Start to explore what happiness means to you. Is it a feeling of peace? Making millions. Being your authentic self. Speaking your truth. Helping others. It's different things for different people. Abundance is 'more than I need' for some people. For others it's wild independent wealth.

For you it could be perfect health. Maybe it's time and freedom and joy. Whatever it is, it's the emotion behind the
intention that gives it power (good or bad, positive or negative). If you can't get a clear picture of what you're doing, try
to get a sense of what you want your life to *feel* like. What
you're trying to tap into is a sense of abundance, a sense of
enoughness.

Here's the hard bit: you have got to feel the emotion
before you actually get the thing. Fake it till you make it.
You are not waiting for the result to make you happy; you
are reaching for happiness in anticipation of the result coming. Whole. Fulfilled. Satisfied, not wanting. You want to get
to a point where you are able to conjure those feelings and
live in them now, while you're waiting for your 'dream life'
to appear – that is the secret. Sit in certainty that what you
desire is already here. *Feel* yourself in your new home, fill it
with the laughter and love, with memories you're yet to create. Spend time imagining it in great detail, building a rich
picture. Make yourself feel like it's already happened. When
you properly connect you will feel wild gratitude, a love for
life, creative flow, joy for existence and when you feel all
those things you won't be looking for something in the
future that is yet to arrive. You'll already have everything
you need. And ironically the things you thought you needed
will start to stream into your life with ease.

Move

Shake a leg! There has got to be some action too so, once you've connected with what you want, it's time to move. I had been 'in the zone' for donkey's, visualising my little heart out daily, eyes on a bigger prize. I was still working as an assistant to a personal shopper and out of the blue got asked to do a TV interview (as a fashion 'expert'), alongside a panel chatting about dresses on the Oscars Red Carpet when that still felt like an appropriate use of one's time! It was totally left field, I had never done anything in telly before so immediately I said yes.

While sitting, live, on an unbearably uncomfortable high stool talking about Drew Barrymore's powder-blue gown and bird's-nest hair, something clicked. I realised that TV had been a desire or a quiet ambition I had buried. There had been flickers of 'that would be cool' but it was so far from where I was and what I saw around me that it seemed impossible so I just never entertained it. Even still, after getting the tiniest taste for it, I felt, on almost every level, that it was a ridiculous pursuit but I loved the whole machine, behind the scenes, the production, the energy, the idea of us all working to one goal, telling a story, offering escape, entertaining. On paper I believed this was something frivolous, me looking for attention (literally), but my soul felt so bloody excited that I couldn't ignore it! knew I had to at least give it a shot or I would regret never having tried.

I had no idea how to move into TV but I started. I emailed agents cold, I knocked on doors, I offered to make tea, I came up with ideas, I pitched stories and doors started to open. As if by magic, things started to come to me – chance meetings in cafes, random responses from an agent who in theory should never have entertained me, beautiful introductions, help from strangers with influence. It felt easy. There was a tonne of rejection too, raised eyebrows and subtle smirking, but I was oblivious. There was an EASE to it all and that ease was a signal that I was on the right path. So I kept going! I didn't really know at the time but those nights spent dreaming about being interviewed on a chat show, properly feeling into what it would be like to sit on that stage, really imagining myself in it, meant the lines between what was real and imagined started to blur! Call it coincidence, maybe it would have happened anyway, but I don't really believe in coincidence. In a short space of time I found myself on that set being interviewed about my very first TV documentary.

So make a start, show some intention, begin to see opportunities and take a leap. And just wait for your world to change.

"The bad news is you're falling through the air, nothing to hang on to, no parachute. The good news is, there's no ground"

Chögyam Trungpa

White Flag

So you're now crystal clear on what you want, you're spending time with your future self every day and your eyes are wide open. So what next?

Chill the fuck out.

Here's the truth, or at least my version of it! None of us really have a clue what this life is all about. We landed on earth without a manual and we are blindly stumbling through, looking at each other with wide eyes and terror, hoping that someone knows the gig. The blind leading the blind. It's terrifying to admit that outright, to say out loud that we have no idea, that we have no control. Zero!

But what if we walked *into* that feeling instead of away. What if we recognised that there's no parachute, accepted that and enjoyed the free fall? Imagine knowing that there is something bigger at play, there is a plan and a path for us and all we have to do is *allow*. Imagine not having to push every single day. To plan and obsess and fixate on what next and what if? Imagine sitting down, wrapping yourself in a soft duvet, and allowing yourself to just *be*.

The word 'surrender' conjures up images of white flags and defeat, a battle lost, but surrender is really about faith in something bigger than you. A belief that you are being guided, that there is a bigger plan for you. Some people call it God. Universe, Gaia, Source, Higher Self . . . it's not important what you call it but what *is* important is that you give in to it. That you allow yourself to be held by something greater than all of us. That's not to say you write your list, sit at home in your knickers eating nachos and wait for the BAFTA but rather that you relax into a state of knowing that what you deeply desire is coming to you and all you have to do is line up. Line up and then show up. Easier said than done to be fair but we're up for it!

Surrender is something I must work at, constantly. I am wildly impatient; 'walk before I could crawl' impatient. I have spent years cursing myself for not knowing things, not knowing all the things, feeling like I'm missing a detailed map that everyone else has. I have an idea in my mind, I can see myself there on a stage, in a house by the sea, with a beautiful little family (my own, obviously!), surrounded by love and brilliant humans helping me grow and glow. I'm glam as fuck in this vision (obviously); I'm in a kimono and drinking Martinis and my hair is down to my arse and there's not a split end in sight . . . you get the gist. I'm there; in my mind I'm already there but when do I actually get there? This game is boring. I'm ready. This isn't working. But it *does* work, when you trust and stop trying to control every single thing – and I know this because I've experienced exactly that.

I once asked my dear friend Maurice (also my hair stylist): 'How can I get my hair to grow long?' His response, deadpan like only he can: 'Stop cutting it'! Which makes total sense but it requires patience and care and time and belief that it will eventually get there. I will eventually get there. I cannot will it to grow quicker, I cannot pay it to hurry up, I can't seduce it with a promise and a smile. I just have to wait. And trust. Trust that it will come when it's good and ready. And you have no doubt, not an ounce that if you stop cutting your hair it will grow. That same certainty now needs to be applied to other areas of your life.

Obviously I could get extensions and the length of my hair is not that central to my life and well-being but it's an example I think of often and I try to apply this sense of trust and knowing to the more important things in my life. The things I want with all my heart even when I'm trying to play it cool. I am loath to admit that I can't force someone to give me my dream job in the perfect location at the exact time that I am free. I cannot schedule having a baby. I cannot time it 'perfectly', I have had to wait and trust that if it was meant to be it would come in time . . .

"Stop interfering with your growth. Stop trying to control it. You don't berate a seed for its inability to bloom overnight. You do not poke or prod it into growing faster. You feed it, nourish it, water it and trust that it will blossom, in its own time. And it does"

Me!

I have never valued the art of restraint. It feels weak, unambitious. But to surrender isn't to give up altogether but to give up on your idea of a 'perfect timeline'. The universe does not respond to your impatience, it doesn't care about your diary, it give zero fucks about the idea you have around what should be done NOW. It knows that things unfold in a way that is right. 'Divine timing'. Annoying as hell until you realise that the unfolding is in line with your readiness. Read that again. Things happen when you are ready, rejection and frustration are just steering you in the right direction.

Your impatience only serves to block you from receiving the very things you desire. Your impatience creates resistance. It suggests you don't have trust. You are not 100% sure that you will get what you want if it's left to someone/something else. But there is something beautiful in handing over the reins and taking a nap. A gardener does not plant a seed and harass it into growing. If she did, it wouldn't make the seed grow any faster. A gardener plants a seed – carefully, thoughtfully, gently – then she leaves it, knowing that, when the time is right, the little seed will emerge. It will emerge effortlessly and elegantly – no pressure, no forcing.

"The physical body is at work every moment, an array of mechanisms with a brilliance of design and efficiency our human efforts have never begun to match. Our hearts beat, our lungs breathe, our ears hear, our hair grows. And we don't have to make them work – they just do. Planets revolve around the sun, seeds become flowers, embryos become babies, and with no help from us. Their movement is built into a natural system. You and I are integral parts of that system, too. We can let our lives be directed by the same force that makes flowers grow – or we can do it ourselves"

Marianne Williamson, *A Return to Love*

Freak

'We hear it a lot now: 'I am a control freak.' It's announced with a slightly stifled pride and worn as a badge of honour. A 'control freak' in my mind was someone with an eye for detail, a relentless work ethic, a laser-focused drive towards success. It's kind of cute. Or at least that's what I thought.

But being a 'control freak' can have a pretty negative effect. Micromanaging every tiny thing leaves very little space, in your brain, your mind, your energy. And as you'll know if you've ever rented, space is always at a premium. We may want to manifest like a beast but if there's no space or time in our lives for new experiences, if we're so exhausted from relentlessly running, we won't even see the opportunities. If we refuse to allow room in our day and in our life, the things we want on a deep level will just pass us by and we're too busy replying to emails about nothing.

But what's the alternative? Doing nothing? We've been taught that adulthood means action, activity, a white-knuckle grip. We are supposed to be doing something. ANYTHING! Go out and get a job, look busy, make it happen, take the bull by the curly horns. We're taught that this level of control is the route to success. Big businessmen know everything and this is what they do so this must be the way. Except we all know how that ends.

When you're in the grip of that masculine, aggressive energy of 'just getting shit done', the last thing you want to be told is to 'chill out'. It's infuriating. It's affronting. What does 'go with the flow' even mean? There is so much to do, time is running out, your neighbour has already made the 30 under 30 list, you're still in a rental, your 'side hustle' is drying up and your eggs are starting to shrivel ... there is no goddamn time to CHILL OUT.

This impatience, and the assumption that you have to do it all yourself, immediately sends a punchy signal to the Universe that you do not trust. You don't trust anyone. You don't trust yourself to share responsibility, to lead. You don't trust others to perform. You don't trust the Universe to *provide*. So, you can stick stuff on a vision board till the cows come home but the energetics of your actions speak more loudly than any board ever will.

The alternative is to slow down, get conscious and surrender. It may sound lazy and risky but there is power in being passive too. A quiet, knowing strength and a solid belief that things are working out for you and that you are being looked after no matter what madness is right in front of you or how far away your 'dream life' seems. It's coming and there is relief in that knowing.

Balance!

An overdose of 'male' energy is macho, aggressive, controlling, forceful and unnatural but, for the most part, this is the vision of what success looks like. It comes dressed in this suit; we have got to 'make it happen'. So we all ramp up the masculine, we become hard, pushy and deeply competitive. You must fight to win and there is only ever one winner.

The feminine, by contrast, is more passive. It doesn't *do* anything; it is not fixated on the doing. It is quiet, open and receptive but this shouldn't be mistaken for weakness. Feminine energy when consciously cultivated is madly magnetic. There is no need to fiercely 'go out and get it'; it is about attraction and magnetism.

My whole working life, I was a 'doer'; my instinct is still to do, do, do. Relentless in my capacity to pitch and produce, I thought that, if I didn't do it, it would never get done. If I didn't push and shout and move forward, I would disappear; opportunities would vanish. It didn't matter which direction I was going in, there was no time to consider such things. On and on and up and away. Away from myself and my purpose (whatever that is). The movement felt natural, it was all I knew. To sit and wait was suicide. I would cease to be and I would have done it to myself.

Then 2020 arrived. I had been dabbling with a slow-down for a while, talking about it in loose terms, testing what it felt like, playing with the idea. But I could never bring myself to fully commit. It can take a long time to walk away from the path you know, even if you're sure it's not headed the right way. I was exhausted and having achieved loads of things I wanted, I still felt uneasy and dissatisfied. I felt like I had built myself a hamster wheel and the only way to survive was to keep moving my little legs as fast as I could. Then a small global pandemic halted production. The government forced me to stay at home. To *be* at home. And while it wasn't exactly rest, it was very much welcomed, which took me by surprise.

Someone had finally saved me from myself and my to-do list. I had just started recording a chat show (my dream job), I had a new series in the works, my podcast due for release; 2020 was a deliciously round and hopeful number, it was supposed to be a BIG one. Our big one, and it *was*, just not in the way I imagined. For the first time in my entire adult life, I had nowhere to go. Routine, which I'd sneered at – something for office bores and squares – was forced upon me and, within those confines, I could finally move freely. I felt safe in the inaction, comfortable with this consistency thing.

In our homely little prison, I found a sense of peace that I had travelled the world in search of. I finally surrendered. I allowed myself to be taken, handcuffed, to that carpeted cell, out for a daily walk with no certainty around my release date – but in that cell there was stillness that made me feel full.

We were away from family. The first time since we moved where we couldn't make a quick trip back to Ireland. There was sickness and near-death, devastating relationship breakdowns, milestone marriage celebrations, worry and fear, but also togetherness. We were separate from all of it, on a pontoon looking back but never quite able to reach dry land. When the lockdown was first announced, my gut instinct was to run, to run 'home'. Home to my family and familiarity and a land that felt protected, it felt safe, but that wasn't practical and so we dared ourselves to stay, to sit it out (or in) and see what happened. What happened was a new family was born. My own little family.

I started to meditate every day (five minutes to begin with), multiple times some days – 'mainlining' meditation as a means of maintaining my sanity. I willed myself to see the wonder in this the weirdest of situations. I let go of my disappointment about the show, I didn't know when I would work again but I knew it was out of my control. In those unexpected moments, I realised that what I had been chasing was there all along. I had enough. I had everything I ever needed in our rented house in London. The insatiable hunger I had felt seemed to disappear and I realised I would survive even if I didn't do all of the things I was so desperately chasing as a way of justifying my worth. If they didn't happen (EVER) I would be OK. I wouldn't die of shame or embarrassment; I wouldn't be a failure. I am not what I do, I just am. If all I have now is all I ever have then that would be enough.

I began to experiment again with 'creating' in my mind. Writing a different kind of list. I would sit and allow this new version of myself and my future to wash over me. Dr Joe Dispenza would reverberate in my ears ... 'What would it feel like if your prayers had already been answered?' I wasn't thinking of a shiny show or a house by the sea. I found myself crying (perhaps some repressed terror at the ending of the world but on I went). They already had. The thing, the people I had been running from my whole life, were still there and finally I could feel it.

I want for nothing. I have everything I need. I am safe. I am fed. I am whole. I am thankful I have arrived in this place when I tried for so long to drive myself off the edge. Thank you.

Chapter Eight

Your Subconscious is a Little Bitch

Your subconscious/unconscious mind is where you store your beliefs. It's the lens through which you see the world and all its possibilities (and limitations). Like a filing cabinet, it holds a record of everything you've seen or experienced and makes sense of the world based on these. You may not actually see it but it is driving everything until you do. Down there in the recesses of your mind is where your blocks exist, your limiting beliefs, the things you tell yourself on a loop. They require zero effort; they are automatic, which is great, because it frees you up to use your brain for challenging things that require engagement. New, exciting things or difficult things. The subconscious takes care of the day-to-day stuff.

But the issue is, you didn't choose what's looping in there. Like a computer with games already installed, you have to play what you've got and deal with it. Maybe you wouldn't have chosen Grand Theft Auto if you had been consulted; you may have gone for something less aggressive, less survival, more peaceful and hopeful and certain. But you got Grand Theft Auto because that's what was available at the time and no one really knew if it would have an impact and everyone was just doing the best they could with what they knew. It's all part of the human journey but you're still stuck in Grand Theft Auto so what now? That idea that your past experience shapes your future – 'show me the boy at seven and I'll show you the man' – can feel bleak and very final, like the ending was written before you had a chance to start reading.

And, in fairness, you can read all the books and arm yourself with the tools, but they generally focus on the conscious mind rather than accessing the blocks that live beneath the surface in the subconscious. You can get it intellectually, understand and want with all your heart to change your life, but it won't stick until you get mucky. Until you decide to dig around down there and unearth all of the programming that has been holding you back. Stuff you learned when you were a kid that gave you an idea about how the world works. And it serves you, until it doesn't.

Tune In

The subconscious left unquestioned is a little bitch. Useful no doubt, historically! Her intention has been to keep you safe, to make sure you survive in the wild. But you're not in the wild any more, and mostly you are safe, you are thriving – you don't need her naggy little voice poking at you daily. Become aware of her nudges. Her condemnation of you and others. Her dismissal of your goals and desires. She is the one who tells you to stay in bed when you promise yourself you'll go for a run. She tells you it's fine to do it tomorrow and that actually what you need is sleep and, in that moment, she is a saviour. She gives you permission to flake and to check out of your plans and/or responsibilities but that metaphorical lie-in comes at a cost.

When you listen to her and obey her without question or awareness, you reinforce her voice and your dependence on her. On a deep level, she is reminding you that you're not good enough, you never really stick at things, that body is never going to be yours and you probably wouldn't have got the job anyway. She taps into and preys on the most vulnerable parts of you. She takes advantage of the bits of you confined to the shadows, the bits of you you wish didn't exist. In ignoring them you hope they'll disappear, but they embed even deeper and by keeping them in the dark they become your dirty little secret. Shrouded in shame and hiding, your subconscious plays you, mocks you and keeps you small. She ensures that the dreams you have at night as you drift off, and the plans you devise when you are buoyant, make you feel foolish the next day. You are not capable and it's embarrassing that you ever thought you were.

So, you stay quiet. Your plans remain in your mind or in the middle of a notebook you pray no one will ever find and your subconscious keeps you and your ridiculous desires for a big life safe; she swallows them whole. She's protecting you from yourself. From being the fullest embodiment of yourself. You will never fail as long as she keeps you where you are because you will never try. That is her power and it will remain that way until you tackle that bitch to the ground and take it back. It was yours all along.

Voices in My Head

OK, sorry, maybe I got a bit aggressive there, and, to be fair, she means well. You stay small, she is successful. You stay in your comfort zone. No one gets hurt. But you didn't come here to play small; that's not the plan. So, one way or another, she needs to shut up or you need to figure out why she's chatting shit. The only way that happens is if you recognise her voice in the moment.

I used to think I had voices in my head, in a way that might be worrying for some people. Then I started to really engage with them and make friends with them and they became less powerful and less dominant. I named these different aspects of me that until then had lurked in the shadows. They're still there; I call them 'little bitches'. They are a team, a crew, a squad but although they lodge in my granny flat (that is not a euphemism), they're not my kind of women.

One of them, **The Sneer**, likes to ruin things all the time. She's snide and judgemental – of other people, of me, of how I behave, of my most intimate moments. She laughs at me for trying new things and goads me when I mess up. She thinks I'm naive for being hopeful and finding good in people, in situations. She's the one who says 'I told you so' and rolls her eyes at your deep desire for happiness. 'Don't be so ridiculous, most people are not happy, it's an illusion.' She thinks you're stupid. She sniggers at you while you weed the garden or 'build' pizza with your kids – who do you think you are? Seriously. The job is to hear her, see her and recognise her as someone separate from yourself. She is not your friend. She's an asshole. She takes beautiful moments and reduces them to rubble.

The Task-Master. Oh, this one is a piece of work, literally. She pushes me relentlessly. She works me to the bone and fills me with fear when things are quiet. 'It's done; good while it lasted.' She denied me a maternity leave and reminds me that I will be replaced as soon as I stop. She pushes me to produce, like a line manager on a conveyor belt. She is ruthless and unforgiving. She denies me time off, embarrasses me when I take a break or run out of steam, makes me pretend I don't miss anyone or anything and she makes me work like I am a machine without a heart or a need or any limits whatsoever. Now, if she showed up like this I would obviously be wary, I wouldn't really want to hang out with her, but she's seductive, she's glossy and self-assured. She promises me I can be the same if I just keep going. And she rewards me, to be fair. When I obey her I am gifted; with cash and accolades and praise. But what I lose is much more valuable. I make her wear a hairnet now and tell her to fuck off when I want to FaceTime my daughter on a job or take a nap or just do nothing. She is not the boss of me!

The Robot. She doesn't feel anything. She is cold and hard and self-sufficient. Disconnected. She likes the idea of family holidays, nourishing friendships and intimacy but the fear of need pushes her to dismiss their value. She is so scared of needing people that she convinces me I don't. The fear of recognising how much she longs for and loves these things is too scary to hold onto. What if someone dies or rejects or abandons? These frilly things are a bonus but they're not necessary and they leave her open; they make her feel weak. Connection comes at a cost to The Robot when she would rather plough on. Dry your eyes. Detach from people who you love because you might lose them or miss them. If you never really commit then it'll be easier in the end when they disappoint with their human ways. She means well, that poor metal wench, she wants only to mind me and save me the pain of heartache. She freezes my heart to help me but she denies me connection, experience, warmth and love.

The '*Mé Féinner*' (an Irish term that translates directly to 'me for myself' but basically means someone who looks after themselves first/always and not in a 'Self-care

Sunday' kind of way). It can be easier or at least more tolerable to explore the parts of yourself that are tough, but
mostly tough on you. It's less comfortable to reveal the bits
of you that are tough on everyone else. The self-serving
parts. The '*Mé Féinner*' is greedy and looks out for herself
first and foremost: 'What's in it for me?'; 'How do I benefit?'
She can be overruled but she can also rear her head after
you've done something without a motive; she'll suggest
you've been taken for granted, that you're a fool. She
quickly cuts people off if they don't play by her rules (there
are quite a lot of rules and no one ever really knows about
them but her). She is impatient and disinterested if you
can't 'do' anything for her but she is very resistant if anyone
else asks her to do something for them. She uses people,
believing everyone is replaceable. Keep moving, keep dancing, keep going. On and up. Up and away. She turns life
into an impossible hard game that leaves me feeling guilty
and empty.

Now, Bev is a hoot. **Beverly** (**Hills**) officially. She's a
badass, the one who told me aged six that when I grow up
I'll be a 'business woman in a turquoise convertible with my
hair blowing in the wind.' She is ambitious. She is wildly
ambitious. She will make you believe you can do anything
and everything. You *must* do everything. Wind in your sails,
her in your ear, you're invincible! Average success is not of

interest to her. If it's not BIG, she's immediately off to the next. She gets frustrated when everything she wants (and she wants everything) doesn't arrive yesterday. She doesn't want to wait. She doesn't want to do things for fun; hobbies are for wasters yet she resents those who have them, and sniggers at 'the simple life.' If things don't 'come easy' she abandons them, convincing her fragile little self that she never wanted them anyway. Every minute must be spent creating a gloriously enviable life that makes Bev feel absolutely superior and less self-conscious about her underlying fear that she's actually a bit crap at everything. She puffs her chest, sprays her hair and gets in the car but she always forgets the kid.

Kimono Kim (a second cousin once removed of Beverly). She is the most glam of them all. She wears vintage robes and drinks Martinis for tea while weeding in her bare feet. She is earthy and sexy and deliciously self-assured. She's outrageously confident and very magnetic. Things come very easily to Kimono Kim, so what's the problem? Well, she's pretty unforgiving. Her focus and obsession with how she appears and how people see her means she's pretty self-absorbed. She's also a pain in the arse perfectionist. Nothing is ready; nothing is good enough. Good enough is not good enough. She demands that the best side is always out. She shuts the door on the messiness of my mind and my life; no one is allowed past a certain point. She believes that if people ever saw the 'real' me – the sloth-like, tired, frazzled, frightened me – that they will bolt. People love Kimono Kim because she's a bit fab but she's guarded and shallow and she forgets that she's most loveable when her lipstick is not quite right and she's singing (badly) to The Cranberries, when she puts on her pyjamas and lets people into her messy house.

That's my gang. There are more, of course, and I will probably always be discovering them. Some are easier to live with than others – a couple are so ruthlessly destructive that it feels like a full-time job just keeping them in check – but they are controllable. They are aspects of me, they are not me. If I can see them, I am not them and so it is my job to remain aware of the behaviours they drive and decide if I'm being given a bum steer or falling back into age-old habits that leave me cold. Sometimes even when you're committed to calling them out, they pop up when you least expect. Remind yourself that the inner critic is fear gone wild and give yourself a break. You can resume, you will be fine, you can flourish.

Identify the 'characters' in your mind who are driving your behaviour on a deep level and try to get a handle on them – this may take ages or you may already have them ringing in your ears. Name them, dress them up, give them dimensions and shape. Then shut those bitches down when you hear their chatter. Recognise the voice, identify the character and reason with her. Ask her questions, call her bluff, drill down on what she says, the assumptions she makes. Do they nourish you or deprive you? Are they true or are they bullshit? Real or imagined. These voices, these characters, are a part of you, a part of you that, until now, you may not have been consciously aware of. See her and name her. Bring her into the middle of the room, shine a big flood light on her and let her speak – her fears and notions and non-truths. Then decide in the light whether what she is offering will help you or hold you back.

Chapter Nine

Get Into Your Body

Remember that you can keep a gratitude journal, stay in the present, post colourful Instagram pictures, burn all the incense and sit in mediation, but if you're a dick when you step out into the real world, what's the point? People can use their spirituality as just another way to separate themselves from others. To feel superior and special. Do meditation not to get good at meditation but to get good at life. In life, not at home on your mat. Embrace spirituality to grow, to see more clearly and to flourish, not to distance yourself from people.

The space that you give yourself in meditation is not about escaping the world for 10 minutes, it's about connecting with yourself and allowing room in your life to hone the conversation with yourself – not the noise and chatter of thoughts but the deeper dialogue that is only heard in the space between. Quiet the mind and the heart can speak. Our minds, bless them, they're hyperactive little ones. Yes, they offer some good advice at times and can be quite clever too, but Jesus, they never shut up. It's all 'me, me, me' and when you quiet your mind, it will find another way to get your attention. It will get louder the more threatened it becomes, and the quieter you become, the greater the threat. You have got to be ready for that rebellion.

Watch the thoughts from the back seat or, better still, from the sunroof looking in; up there you'll get a clearer view. The idea is to create some distance so you can separate yourself from the thought and the chatter. You are not that. You are the one watching it. Don't attack or attempt to shut her down; the ego is a fragile wench and will bite back. Instead roll your eyes, kick back, laugh, observe without judgement, and then do what you do from a place of choice.

Bird'S-Eye View

When I get the wind in my sails, high on my own supply, caught up in an old story or a belief system, that is my ego at play and, damn, she's persuasive. 'I have been let down or ignored or wronged. I am furious; they are awful, I should never have trusted anyone.' I so easily get whipped up and create a scenario that often isn't reality at all. Now, it's not like I'm totally losing my mind, but, in that frenzied survival state, the prism through which I view everything is cloudy as fuck. It is skewed. It is broken. I am seeing only the actions that support my idea and refusing to see the reality, refusing to see any good at all.

What I try to do is take a step back, to recognise that I've gone into autopilot (TRY is the big word here). When I can, I shift into observing myself (from the sunroof). I am watching this scene unfold and with a little distance I can generally see more clearly. 'Oh, look at me there absolutely FUMING; cute jumper. See how my nostrils flare when I'm raging. Look how panicked I am when I feel overwhelmed, how I assume people can't help; everyone is doing it wrong. See how irate and upset I get when I don't get my own way, when I feel overlooked. It's actually a bit cute from up here although I wouldn't fancy being on the receiving end. What am I furious about again?' Once you start to observe your behaviour from a different point of view – patterns will start to emerge. Don't berate yourself, welcome them and be open to what you can learn. Also acknowledge that you are aware of it right now.

I started to observe a pattern at home every time I made dinner. My intention was to do something nice and spend some quality time with my little family but I always seemed to get hijacked, by myself. I would volunteer to make said dinner, I'd be in the kitchen happily listening to a podcast or some music, really enjoying preparing food for my little crew. But the closer I got to serving the food, the more annoyed I would become: 'He's taking the piss; I'm in here slaving away and they're watching telly. What are they laughing at? Why is there no coconut milk!? The least he could do is set the table. What are they doing in there? Why are they having fun and I'm stuck in here mak-ing dinner like a fifties housewife. I'm sick of this. I told them it was ready. Why is he ignoring me? This is SO RUDE. They can eat it or not, I don't even care any more.' This mad torrent of thoughts crashing into my sweet little set-up – goading me to blow things up. It was physical, the rage was furious, seething, spitting, unexplainable and completely irrational.

I would serve dinner with a side of resentment, my husband completely unaware of the screaming toddler inside, bemused and confused by my sudden change in mood.

I managed to gate-crash my little rage fest one evening. I felt the swell coming in to take me over, to ruin our evening together, to rob me of the intimacy and joy I get from feeding those I love. When the familiar heat began to rise in my chest and the chatter became louder, the accusations more incriminating, I told myself this: 'Honey, you offered to make dinner; you actually like doing it and not that we're counting but it's definitely your turn! It's fab to be able to pour some love and intention into a meal that your family will enjoy. You don't need to ask him to set the table; the food isn't ready yet so you can do that. You're just trying to control a bit and that's cool – it's you, it's fine – but it doesn't make for an easy evening. This podcast is good and you've got another 10 minutes to just enjoy it while they watch *Paw Patrol*! Relax. They're not leaving you out. You are not being overlooked. They are not taking advantage. Step back and *choose* to enjoy this evening. PS cute jumper.'

Meditation is not about sitting in prayer for a month; it's about developing the ability to pause. Gifting yourself the space for choice to present itself. Once there's space for that choice, you can make decisions from a place of knowing, responding with intention rather than reacting out of habit. Deepak Chopra says, 'the Higher Self is whispering to you softly in the silence between your thoughts.' If you can quiet the mind, you can hear your higher self whispering and she is a queen who has your back so listen up. Make room for her to whisper and don't be fooled by her gentle approach. The softness is not a lack of confidence, it is an abundance of it. So sure and steady is your inner whisper that it never needs to raise its voice. Hear it like a roar, take it seriously and you will always be supported.

Embodiment

As someone who had an eating disorder, I have had pretty ambivalent feelings about my body for a very long time. It was something to be managed and punished, preened and presented. I was *in* it but it never really fit me; it never provided a place of comfort or rest or safety. As if it was borrowed or I was squatting. I lived on edge, waiting for someone to show up and give me permission to unpack, or for someone to land with keys to a new place, somewhere that might actually feel like home. What both of these situations depended on was intervention from someone other than me. I was waiting for someone to save me!

The sense of not feeling at home in my own skin was heightened when I felt stress or pressure. I remember after being drafted in last-minute to cover a live show for a week. The sense of being out of control or nervous, feeling scared I would mess up, frightened to fail, was too much to bear so I switched my focus to my body. When I sat on the couch, about to go live, it was as if my skin was too small for me! It's hard to articulate but I felt like it didn't fit, there was no comfort, no sense of familiarity or warmth. It was restrictive and tight and irritated. Ready to burst. Of course that wasn't actually my skin but my mind – restrictive, tight, irritated. Afraid of losing control, so shifting focus to the thing I spent my life controlling; my body. But it stayed with me, something niggled for the first time. I felt sad that I couldn't sit comfortably in this vessel, that I couldn't lovingly dress it and express myself through it. I felt guilty realising that I had yet again made it my enemy instead of embracing it as my friend.

Often we spend so much time in our heads – battling, reasoning, chatting, what-if'ing with ourselves – that we are much more comfortable there, even in the tight confines of our skulls. How often during the day do you stop to check in to see how your body actually is? How often do you listen to the niggles or give room for the creaks to creak? Do you override the messages you get from your body in favour of powering through, dismissing the desire and sometimes desperate need for attention, rest or love? After I had my daughter, I felt a shift in my body – no, I felt a shift in the way I *see* my body. I became more forgiving, more compassionate, gentler. I stopped seeing the body, my body, as something foreign that needed to be trained and forced and tamed.

I had to look at how judgemental I had become, not just with myself but with everyone around. I realised my own dysmorphia and the way I related to my body was not just something contained within me; it had spilled out into what I thought of other people. If they didn't have a hard-ened, tight body, it was laziness. In my mind I quickly switched someone with soft curves into someone sloth-like. It's difficult to admit that and it is still difficult to change that in motion. I did not want my relationship with my body, with bodies in general, to leak onto my daughter, to poison her perception.

I wanted her to continue to view herself the way I do, as this beautiful, perfect soul in a spacesuit that helps her to enjoy everything that this human experience has to offer. Her body is something that facilitates her journey through this life; it is her container and her home for as long as she is on this earth. I want her to marvel at its com-plexities and revel in the imperfections; I want her to nurture and nourish it, to push it so she knows her strength and power, to rest it so she feels her strength and power. Her soft chubby legs made me view the softness of the human body in a completely different way. They allowed me to, if not celebrate, then to at least accept the softness in my own body. When I feel the folds of my skin or a bulge that hasn't always been there, I try to look at it with tenderness, to think of how I feel when I run my hand across her little bloated belly, feel her skin and see the rise and fall of her breath, and I apply the same wonder and love I give her to myself. I see how she moves and the joy she gets from discovering and

using her body, and I allow myself to do that too – to rediscover my own body, to unpack my bags for a bit and, as one
of my favourite writers Mary Oliver says, 'breathe into the
soft animal' of my body.

Touch your soft, tired, fleshy bits. Embrace the parts
of you that you often dismiss as repulsive. The cellulite, the
rolls, the dark circles and crow's feet. The bits of you that
tell the story of a life lived. Accept your morning breath as
human, not grotesque. Explore the parts of you that are
imperfect, the bits that are kept in the messy cupboard of
your mind. Open it up. Open yourself up. Lovingly look at
those desperately beautifully human parts of yourself.
Breathe them in . . .

And Breathe ...

There is a lot of chat about breath work and breathing and 'coming back to the breath'; it sounds so easy it's almost boring. Give me the magic pill please and less of the breathing nonsense. It is innate – if you weren't able to do it, you wouldn't be here – but, relearning how to breathe can change how you live in your own body. It becomes a tool that you can use once a day, a hundred times a day, to bring awareness to the now so that you can choose how to perceive a situation or an interaction. It becomes a punctuation mark, a physical pause to ground you in this moment and by operating in this moment alone you are in the driving seat. You override the bit of your mind, your subconscious mind that is on autopilot and relating to something historic. You can also pull back into focus the part of you that catastrophises the future. You are here NOW; you can choose to respond from a new reality rather than a remembered one or a reality that may never materialise. This is awareness – the ability to pause in the moment and have a word with yourself, ask yourself a question and proceed with information rather than an overactive imagination.

Something magical happened when I started to live inside my body rather than in my head. I started to focus on my breath. To drop into my body. To really feel the air enter my belly and fill my lungs, to feel the cool air in through my nose and the warmth of the exhale. The in and out, the up and down, the expansion and contraction. To realise that this act of breathing – this complex mechanical motion that we do without thought from the moment we arrive on this planet – is how we're here! As soon as it stops, we stop. Yet every day we run around unaware, taking for granted the mastery and magnificence just beneath the bonnet of our bodies. We only look up when the engine stalls, when the breath gives up. What if instead of waiting for it to break down we could marvel and appreciate it in the moment.

For me, coming back to my body was about touch. About gently holding myself like I would a child. Psychologist Tara Brach talks about the power of holding your cheek or face and giving yourself the love and compassion you often seek from someone else. Loving yourself back into your body. Falling back in love with your body. This might sound trite and a bit airy-fairy but remind yourself that you are only capable of giving the depth of love to others that you give to yourself.

I decided to develop a relationship with my body that was based on respect. Love felt like a stretch at the time but I figured I could manage some jovial respect. Every morning, I place one hand on my heart to connect and one on my belly to feel the rise and fall, to bring me back. It felt uncomfortable at first, foreign, embarrassing, but over time that changed to comfort and relief. It changed to appreciation. I no longer viewed my body as a vessel to be abused and pushed and tested. I started to fall in love with it. To feel deeply thankful for all the years it has given me, for the moments it danced through pain and ran into the fire, for birthing a baby, for healing, for breathing every single day. For sticking with me while I relentlessly punished it like an inanimate object. For coming back time and time again when I abandoned it. For forgiving me . . .

When I started to nurture it – not just with green juice but with compassion – it began to whisper more loudly to me. It gave me pure stillness and heavy, heady rest; it gave me pleasure without a backseat driver. When I come back to my body and commit to being right here, it always surprises me, winking in acknowledgement of my effort.

Breathe in. Turn attention inwards. Listen. Where does your breath want to take you? What does it want to tell you? When you drift away, come back, attach to the breath and you will land back in your body. Is there something you're trying to avoid? What needs attention? Break down walls and soften the edges. To feel the softness of your body, the velvety in and out of your breath, the up and down of your lungs. The stillness in motion. This is the power of our breath.

Love Letter to My Limbs

It is 2003; I'm in Virginia, America. As the music started, I stood there wondering if my legs would move when the curtain lifted. A part of me secretly hoped they wouldn't. That finally someone might rush in and scoop me off the stage, send me to bed or to hospital or home. Somewhere. But the curtain went up and my legs started to move in time with everyone else, as they had before. Every time before. Like I had been taken over. A lemming. My body wasn't my own, which to be fair was pretty accurate.

It certainly didn't feel like I chose it. It felt uncomfortable. Like the skin didn't fit and my lungs and stomach were made for another vessel. It was wrong and I felt wrong all wrapped up in it. Like an intruder in a fleshy submarine with no idea where we were off to but knowing for sure that I was going the wrong way. My legs were so heavy, like opaque tights – the kind your granny wears but filled with wood not veins. I was solid and stuck, anchored by the weight. And then off we went. My legs betrayed me again. Relentless in their commitment to me, unable to let me down.

I was kind of in awe of their ability to keep going, like the sheer determination to show up every day taunted me, dared me to go further, to push harder, to deny more deeply. My routine was gruelling. It's the kind you hear people undertake when they're transforming into a character and being paid a shedload of money to do it while under strict supervision. I would dance sometimes five shows a day. I drank only black coffee and ate canned pineapple (good for inflammation, or so I was told). If I felt weak I might have an apple, or a box of raisins. I was high. On freedom and the fact that I was unsupervised. I could keep people at arm's-length; they would never really see me. They would never be close enough to see the holes in my story and my insides.

I never thanked my legs for soldiering on or apologised for the relentless withholding. I didn't nourish them or even know them but they always did what I asked without ever making me ask. They're low-key like that. Our bodies are fucking amazing.

Rebel

Rebel with tenderness, with softness and openness and willingness. All the nesses! Rebel with a commitment to see the
light and to fight for it. To search for it in everything and in
every interaction. To walk away from a way of being requires
courage that most of us can't summon every day. There is
comfort in familiar misery. It requires guts and optimism
and hope to change, none of which we can buy. Think of
your heart like a rose; a peony actually. Soft, billowy and
beautiful – the work is to allow the petals to open. When
you think your heart is open, soften it a little more. Allow it
to grow out of your chest, to expand to fill your entire body.
Your heart is not something to be protected behind a shield,
sitting safely under lock and key; it is the source of all your
power, it is your life force and your presence and your
essence. To close your heart and harden yourself in response
to or in anticipation of suffering, is to rob yourself of your
capacity to live fully. The truly brave don't suit up in armour;
they walk naked among us.

Some people will send you flowers and others will
help you bloom. Choose the latter. Always choose the latter.
Choose the one who holds you when you cry angry snotty

desperate tears. When you are wild with fear, choose someone who will hold your hand. Who respects you enough to
know you don't need to be fixed; you need space to grow
and patience while you do it. Someone who is excited, not
threatened, by your growth and your hunger to discover
yourself. Choose someone who observes from a gentle distance as you sway: a flower changing through the
seasons – always in motion. Certain of the return.

*

The Little Thank Yous

Buttery Toast – The kind with holes where lumps of butter drip through onto the plate or your hand and you get to mop it up with the crust. There is something so wildly comforting about this most simple of pleasures. Put it on a gorgeous plate or eat it off some crumpled kitchen roll; it really doesn't matter. The joy is in the oozy, drippy yellow butter and the airy soakage of a good loaf. Together, magic.

A child's laugh! – Hyperactive contagious machine-gun laughter. Bullets of joy spraying all over the shop. Wrinkled eyes and pink gums. Unselfconscious belly laughs that are addictive to provoke: dancing, screaming, blowing raspberries, making the same face or a hundred faces on a loop to get that gift. Children don't laugh to soothe your ego or fill awkward silence. They laugh because you're funny. They are the best audience.

Voice Memos – A long, rambling, slightly incoherent voice memo where a friend paints a picture and gives a running commentary on their current view and general existence. Breathy and excited. Even when you're a million miles away, they're right there and that's kind of lovely!

The smell of a baby's head – You don't even have to own said baby. That oily, powdered innocence. The smell of possibility, of potential. The perfect blank slate. The comforting wholeness and reminder to come back home. The familiarity.

Cups of lukewarm herbal tea.

Flat, warm 7Up – Flat warm 7Up is syrup for the soul. The medicine of your childhood. The gift your mother gave you when you felt sick. Upset stomach, period cramps, broken heart . . . flat warm 7UP is your only man. Not a sign of Fido Dido, that weird little pervert, but the taste of this tonic and the memory of your mother's arms or eyes, her intention, her love. Drink it any day you want. A self-prescribed soul slurp to fix the lot.

Snuggling tight and seeing the world through her waterfall ponytail.

A sliver of cake, held back – a tiny little bit of thought cake from someone who wanted so much to demolish it but loved you more than the sugar rush. Held you in their heads when the buttercream hit their bloodstream and wanted you to love it as much as they did.

Hanging shelves that I bought six months ago.

Poems – Writing them. When was the last time you wrote a poem?! Probably as a kid at school. You don't know where to start, what are the rules, what would you say, where would you even start. Start. Write something. It doesn't have to be good, just truth. Trust that with a little bit of space and an openness to try, you will write something that is pure. And you will feel the pride you did as a six-year-old when your teacher said 'well done'!

Taking off a tight pair of jeans.

A steaming hot two-hour bath – Where your face sweats off and the window fogs up and your fingers turn to wrinkled sausages but you sweat out the stress and you melt just a bit and you let the water hold your tired bones.

A surprise friend – Older. Younger. Different. Wild. Forbidden. New. Falling in love with a friend is one of life's beautiful pleasures. Like falling in love romantically but with none of the games. The raucous laughs and dance while you find your groove. The excitement at meeting a soul you know already but who feels brand new.

A fresh notebook.

Picking a spot – A good one. You know the kind – where there is a root and it just pops out. No mess, no fuss – like it was waiting for you all of its sebaceous little life.

An eye mask – The kind that kills the light altogether but doesn't flatten your face or make your eyebrows itch. It is like a hug for the brain.

Walking on crunchy leaves – Maybe it's more formally known as forest bathing but, before it was commoditised, walking in the woods was just something you did on a Sunday. Steal any day you can, grab an hour or detour so you can feel the soul beneath your feet even for a minute. Crunchy leaves and brittle sticks snapping as you move through the trees and fill your lungs.

Silk pyjamas.

The sea – During lockdown I realised I hadn't seen the sea in six months, maybe more. I felt the pull. A strong primal urge to run but I live in London so it was a bit of a push. I made a promise then; I felt deeply into that want and realised that my dream is to live by the sea. Until that happens, I will never not dip at least my toes in the open sea or marvel at the waves or salute the vastness as I drive on by.

My Ugg slippers.

Holding hands (even though they're dry AF).

Blue Cheese – For breakfast. Stinking and oozing. Served with fresh figs hopping out of their skins and gloopy honey licked from a spoon. Bread to mop it up. Having a 'cheese board' for breakfast is the ultimate act of self-love!

A Face Mask – The cheap ones that go crunchy on your skin and catch around your nose. Green or grey, the kind that make your eyes pop in a picture and cover redness. The ones you're relieved to wash off. The ones that make you grateful that your face still moves.

Freshly washed sheets.

Her face when you pick her up from school.

A green smoothie – Bear with me. The joy of lashing in spinach and nettle powder and nut milk and cold ice to make something that resembles ice cream and means you can eat pasta for the rest of the day.

A giant collar that makes me look half toddler/half priest.

Stream paddling – The cold ferocious water running across your feet until your toes are numb and your soles are sore. Bearing it and the rush of blood that comes when you thaw out! A little sense of achievement for enduring.

Freshly dyed hair!!! – The way it makes your skin pop and the swish.

A 'rich bitch' blow dry.

The fresh smell of the pages and the anticipation of a new book entering into a new story, a new world, a new view.

The rush you get when you book a little trip; the journey, the anticipation and excitement of a break from life to live actual life.

Rubbing her back as she falls asleep purring like a little kitten.

Dancing naked to Florence Welch 'Dog Days Are Over' – a little too close to the window for added danger.

The thrill of a book arriving that you forgot you'd ordered.

Discovering something.

Painting my daughter's nails with turquoise 'finger polish' that smells like the future but also like the past. Holding her juicy little hands still and blowing until that cheap paint is dry. The joy on her face when she shows those fancy nails to anyone who will stop to look.

Watching the fire (it's gas but I don't even care).

A friend in a jumper hand-delivering soda bread that her granny taught her how to make. Wrapped in a chic little parchment parcel and tied with twine.

Getting a bargain!

Watching a kid eat spaghetti – The glorious, unselfconscious messiness of it. The unadulterated commitment to tasting every single mouthful, no ideas about 'appropriateness' . . . just pure enjoyment. In a joy moment.

The conch I got in Key West that I blow to make me feel alive!

Saving for something your soul loves. Something that reminds you of a milestone reached, a goal achieved. Something that makes you feel proud just looking at it.

Turkish Delight.

Builder's Socks – The thick kind that don't itch but feel like a boot. They're hand-knitted, or at least they look that way, with natural dyed yarn and in earthy, homely colours. They remind you of the hills. Of your dad. Of a hearty range in the corner and turf burning. An open door and a kettle always on. They are a promise of home.

A good lip scrub in winter. No one ever achieved their
dreams with chapped lips.

Listening to Marian Keyes' new book.

Melatonin when I can't sleep.

When the sun finds you in a moment when you really need
a reminder that something bigger has your back and it
pops out for a second and light spills in the window and
washes over you and you know things are cool and you
are held.

Red wine from a goblet!

John Tucker Must Die (no judgement).

Cutting up banana skins, soaking them and feeding
the water to my plants.

My Tibetan singing bowl.

Planting seeds with my girl.

Rough grey waves on a ferry to somewhere that feels like
home. Waves so big and foamy and deep that they make
you realise how tiny you are and how futile it is trying to
control things.

An old blanket – One you can't remember buying or getting. It may be moth-eaten or threadbare, but it has wrapped you up in times where comfort was needed. It has sat on your knee patiently while you shuffled to find the perfect position. It has enveloped you on a cold evening while you watched some junk on TV that soothes your soul and lets you escape. It's there like an old, quiet, steady friend. Bringing warmth.

Picking flowers and making bouquets.

A cold shower – 60 seconds – focusing on LONG breaths out.

My neighbours.

Gloopy moreish rice pudding – comfort in a bowl.

A DEEP deep breath – Close your eyes (after you've read this!). Follow your breath through your nostrils, right the way down your throat, through your lungs, feeding your heart into the depths of your stomach. Fill your body with air. Feel it light up every cell and make it new.

The BIG Thank Yous

I don't even know where to start and I'm afraid I'll leave someone out so if I did, THANK YOU, you're my favourite!

Thank you so much to my gang at YMU – Mary, Holly, the two Jades, Sally, Nads . . . and a special shout out to Lizzie who didn't baulk even with some of the admissions in this book. For always being there, gently advising me and reminding me that slow and steady is actually a bit fab. To my literary agent Amanda Harris who is incredible and has lent her support at many wobbly moments – you have guided me gently in what sometimes felt like a mad and overwhelming process. I'll see you in the deep end.

Yvonne Jacob at Ebury for believing in this book and me as a writer from the first paragraph. Your encouragement when I've been needy and controlling and very annoying has been an anchor for me and without your voice memo tutorials on Word this book would not exist outside of my brain. To Marta, Anna, Ellie, Donna and the entire team at Ebury, across publicity, marketing, design – you are the business and I'm so happy to be building something with you.

Megan and Jacob at Carver – you are very clever dreamboats, thanks for helping me bring this book to the world. My therapist Tara, who allows me to make sense of my mind and lighten the load, for holding space and helping me to grow – I am forever grateful.

To Mam and Dad for your endless support and wisdom, for being my compass even when I insisted on driving without a licence. Thank you for being my greatest teachers, I love you deeply. To my sisters – my favourite bitches in the world, thank you for all the laughs, tears and lessons. Michael, Maura and all the gang – for endlessly cheering me on, you are the best adopted family I could ever wish for.

My found family of friends in weird little pockets all over the shop – I love you. Special shout out to Maria for reading and helping with childcare and giving the best advice (and bread) and generally being there via WhatsApp and over too many margaritas.

Roy, the love of my life – thank you for everything, especially our gorgeous little family. You are my number 1, and I am so grateful to have you in my life. I couldn't do anything I do without your unwavering support and your cooking! Thank you for your trust, and for eventually reading the book (if you did, if not no worries) I'll fill you in later.

And finally YOU, for buying up this book or stealing it (I really don't mind). For supporting me or following me on social media, listening to my podcast, watching my shows. It means the world and I'm glad to have you on this joyride! I hope you feel emboldened or inspired or something, I hope you FEEL all the messy feelings that make being human so mad and magical. x

Recommended Reads

- *The How* by Yrsa Daley-Ward (Penguin Books, 2021)

- *A Return to Love* by Marianne Williamson (Harper Thorsons, 2015)

- *Untamed* by Glennon Doyle (Vermilion, 2020)

- *Anam Cara* by John O'Donoghue (Bantam Press, 1999)

- *The Gifts of Imperfection* by Brené Brown (Vermilion, 2020)

- *The 7 Habits of Highly Effective People* by Stephen Covey (Simon and Schuster, 2017)

- *How to Lead a Badass Business from Your Heart* by Makenzie Marzluff (Changemaker Books, 2020)

- *The Secret* by Rhonda Byrne (Simon & Schuster UK, 2006)

- *Conversations with God* (Book One) by Neale Donald Walsch (Hodder and Stoughton, 2008)

- *The Monk Who Sold His Ferrari* by Robin Sharma

- *Wintering* by Katherine May (Rider, 2020)

- *Super Attractor* by Gabrielle Bernstein (Hay House Inc, 2019)

- *The Art of Contemplation* by Richard Rudd (Gene Keys Publishing, 2018)

Your Notes